Employability

Editor: Danielle Lobban

Volume 405

independence
educational publishers

First published by Independence Educational Publishers

The Studio, High Green

Great Shelford

Cambridge CB22 5EG

England

Copyright

Photocopy licence

ISBN-13: 978 1 86168 864 4

Printed in Great Britain

Zenith Print Group

Contents

Introduction

Employability is Volume 405 in the **issues** series. The aim of the series is to offer current, diverse information about important issues in our world, from a UK perspective.

Employability

Youth unemployment has started to rise again after nearly a decade of gradual falls. This book explores employment in the UK and the issues faced by young people looking for employment such as routes into work and employment status. It also looks at ways to prepare for the world of work and how to improve your chances of getting your dream job.

OUR SOURCES

Titles in the **issues** series are designed to function as educational resource books, providing a balanced overview of a specific subject.

The information in our books is comprised of facts, articles and opinions from many different sources, including:

♦ Newspaper reports and opinion pieces

♦ Website factsheets

♦ Magazine and journal articles

♦ Statistics and surveys

♦ Government reports

♦ Literature from special interest groups.

A NOTE ON CRITICAL EVALUATION

Because the information reprinted here is from a number of different sources, readers should bear in mind the origin of the text and whether the source is likely to have a particular bias when presenting information (or when conducting their research). It is hoped that, as you read about the many aspects of the issues explored in this book, you will critically evaluate the information presented.

It is important that you decide whether you are being presented with facts or opinions. Does the writer give a biased or unbiased report? If an opinion is being expressed, do you agree with the writer? Is there potential bias to the 'facts' or statistics behind an article?

ASSIGNMENTS

In the back of this book, you will find a selection of assignments designed to help you engage with the articles you have been reading and to explore your own opinions. Some tasks will take longer than others and there is a mixture of design, writing and research-based activities that you can complete alone or in a group.

FURTHER RESEARCH

At the end of each article we have listed its source and a website that you can visit if you would like to conduct your own research. Please remember to critically evaluate any sources that you consult and consider whether the information you are viewing is accurate and unbiased.

Useful Websites

www.gov.uk

www.graduatecoach.co.uk

www.if.org.uk

www.independent.co.uk

www.inews.co.uk

www.nationalcareers.service.gov.uk

www.parliament.uk

www.politics.co.uk

www.savethestudent.org

www.stepstowork.co.uk

www.successatschool.org

www.targetcareers.co.uk

www.theconversation.com

www.theguardian.com

www.themix.org.uk

www.wearencs.com

www.youthemployment.org.uk

What is employability?

Employability is about having strong soft skills and a professional attitude, as well as relevant qualifications. Here's how school students can become more employable for the job market of the future.

Employability can be defined as the skills, knowledge and attitudes that help people to get a job and to move between jobs. The 'knowledge' aspect and job-specific skills may seem the most concrete and receive the most attention – for example in terms of what qualifications are required for a particular job. However, while it's important for applicants to meet any specific qualification requirements for a vacancy (for example subject, level of study or grades) this isn't ultimately what will get them hired.

Candidates' soft skills, attitudes and experiences outside the classroom, combined with their level of research into the job and employer, are what make them stand out from others with similar qualifications. Employers' recruitment processes typically focus on assessing these, to see what candidates can offer beyond the subjects and grades listed on their initial application. And given that the qualification requirements for many roles are fairly broad – for example a 2.1 degree in any subject, or two A levels at grade A* to C – there will often be a lot of eligible applicants.

Employability skills

Employability skills – aka transferable skills or soft skills – include the following:

♦ commercial awareness
♦ communication
♦ teamwork
♦ negotiation and persuasion
♦ problem solving
♦ leadership
♦ organisation
♦ perseverance and motivation
♦ the ability to work under pressure
♦ confidence.

Why are employability skills important? The future job market

Looking towards the job market of the future, it's soft skills and appropriate attitudes that are likely to remain in demand, long after the market for a particular body of knowledge or technical skill has disappeared. You may have heard the term 'fourth industrial revolution', referring to the merging of physical and digital worlds and concurrent automisation of even relatively skilled white-collar jobs. Of course, no one knows which jobs will stay, go or emerge over the next 20 or 30 years, but it seems likely that there will still be demand for workers with very 'human' skills such as communication or leadership while areas such as numerical or process-driven work can be automated.

First steps to employability

The good news is that many school students will already be developing the skills they need to get hired and remain employable in a changing job market, be it through ironing out a disagreement among hockey team members or plucking up the courage to talk to prospective pupils and their parents as a student rep at a school open evening. All sorts of activities can help develop the right skills and attitudes, so, if they're not already doing so, simply getting involved in something that interests them outside the classroom is a great first step. And reflecting on past experiences may uncover a bank of skills they didn't know they had.

Employability matters for university-bound students

Becoming employable is a pressing matter for students who want to start work straight after school rather than go to university. However, there's no dodging the matter for those who want to get a degree first. They'll still need to find work eventually, and would be well advised to start building their skills as soon as possible.

Some career sectors have recruitment timetables that involve students applying for internships or other forms of work experience in their first or second year of university, so they may have to draw on experiences gained while still at school on their applications. Additionally, at university they may find that it is easier to build their employability through extracurricular activities or part-time work if they already have related experience from their school-days – for example their chances of getting onto a university sports team are likely to be higher if they've already trained hard in that sport while at school. And of course employability depends on similar skills and experiences to those that will impress universities on a UCAS personal statement.

Students applying for apprenticeships or other school leaver programmes may well need to showcase their skills and other experience in the application and interview process. For example, they may be asked to provide evidence that they have the skills or attributes the employer2 seeks in online application forms or at interview.

Your future job doesn't exist yet

The world is changing, and fast. It's thought that lots of jobs you'll go on to do don't even exist yet. So what sort of roles can you expect from the future? And how can you prepare for them?

How things are now

You might think the best jobs to get into are all tech-related (and some are!), but a surprising number are hands-on and people focused. Here are some of the top on and offline roles with a lot of scope to expand in the future.

Healthcare Worker

As we live longer, nurses, doctors and physical therapists are going to be even more in demand. Medical research roles like Epidemiologists (scientists who look into causes of disease and injury) will become vital as the population booms. Similarly, mental health is top of the agenda, so if you think you'd be a counsellor or therapist, it's a great idea. Typically you need a Bachelor's degree for most things medical, but not always.

Software Developers

Apps, websites and games all require programmers to code, test and develop their platforms. From writing computer languages like Java and C++ to devising hacker-proof security systems, developers work across all industries and can be paid really well. Depending on how technical the role is, you might need a relevant degree, but not necessarily. Either way, it's never too late to learn some new digital skills.

Engineers and Technicians

Got a technical mind and love problem solving? The engineers and technicians of the future will be dealing with all sorts of fascinating issues: renewable energy solutions, 'smart' home appliances and space exploration to name but a few! Often the way into these industries is through apprenticeships, but make sure to check out your options.

Plumbers and Electricians

As we move towards more of a freelance economy, there's never been a better time to be your own boss. And the great news? You don't need to go to university to have a rewarding career in most of these areas. In fact, apprenticeships and work experience are a great way to go.

Creative Roles and Project Management

Like schedules and organising? Or more of a freethinking ideas person? While some roles may be taken over by computer systems, people will always be needed to come up with the original concepts, tell them what to do and how to do it. Writing, designing, marketing, managing – all these skills have a place in the future.

Local Artisans

Some things you just can't automate. With more of a drive towards sustainability, cutting back on plastic and locally-produced goods, entrepreneurs can do really well by embracing an ethical angle and offering something the mass market can't. Add to this the advances in social media that allow small businesses to be discovered globally, and you've got a lot of power in locally-grown, locally-made products.

Future-proof your career

We've all heard the headlines: ALL HUMANS REPLACED BY ROBOTS BY 2020! AHH! Well, don't worry, that *probably* won't happen. Although we can't deny that a lot of roles will certainly have some element of increased automation over the next few years. So how do you make sure the computers don't snatch up your future career?

Soft skills

People will always be needed to do the things machines can't. These qualities will put you in good stead whatever industry you end up working in, and, particularly if you move around. The main skills are things like:

- Empathy and Communication – Humans don't just require the efficiency and accuracy of algorithms, but kindness, consideration and understanding too
- Critical Thinking – Technology can predict variables, but we still need humans to make thought-through, informed decisions
- Creativity – AI is great, but it can't produce beautiful paintings, delicious recipes or your favourite Harry Potter book
- Strategic Thinking – Computers can map the small-scale stuff, but not the big overview
- Physical Skills – A robot football team just wouldn't be as exciting as the real thing, would it?
- Imagination and Vision – They might come close, but machines will never have our full capacity to dream and invent. For that, you need the real thing

Where things are heading...

And if that doesn't sound science fiction enough for you, here's a list of jobs that don't exist yet, but might do:

- Mind-Transfer Specialist
- Custom Body Part Engineer
- Robotic or Holographic Avatar Designer
- Gene Designer for Babies and Pets
- Pharmaceutical Artisan
- Extinct Species Revivalist

Fancy bringing back T-Rex, anyone?

9 August 2019

6 ways young people can boost their employability

Experts advise on how to stand out from the crowd when job hunting.

By Katie Wright

With the International Labour Organization warning it will take years before labour markets recover from the huge blow dealt by the pandemic, it's more important than ever to optimise your chances if you're searching for work.

For young people looking to get a foot on the career ladder, education isn't the only way to impress potential employers. These days firms are looking for more than just qualifications and top exam grades.

To mark World Youth Skills Day (July 15), we asked industry experts for their advice on how young jobseekers can make their CVs stand out.

1. Update your social media profiles

'When employers are looking into a candidate to potentially fill a role, part of their research process will often include checking out the candidate's social media profiles,' says Sarah-Jane McQueen, general manager of CoursesOnline.

Your first step should be 'removing anything from your public pages that might be embarrassing or compromising.' Next, consider creating a profile on a professional platform such as LinkedIn: 'Employers are increasingly using the platform to identify potential recruits and want an easy to access overview of your prior experience and useful skills.'

2. Research the role

'Preparation and research can be one of the single most important factors to consider,' says Darren Jaffrey, general manager EMEA and APAC at HireVue, which is why you should always tailor your applications instead of firing off the same CV and cover letter for every job ad.

'Take a detailed look at the company website and the job description, and consider how any previous experience that you have, and your education, might have provided you with relevant skills.'

3. Practise interview questions

Interviews can be incredibly nerve-wracking, especially when you haven't done many before, so ask a friend or family member to help you practise some typical questions.

Jaffrey recommends using the 'STAR' approach when answering questions about your aptitude or experience: 'Include thoughts about the "Situation" you faced, the "Task" at hand, the "Activity" you undertook, and the "Results" achieved (STAR) of your work. This is a great way to organise your thoughts, and offer a detailed response that truly showcases your skills and experience.'

4. Top up your tech skills

'According to research from LinkedIn 150 million new technology jobs will be created in the next five years; however, a 2020 report by the World Economic Forum found that 39% of the UK didn't have the digital skills required to match this demand,' says Mike Davies, COO and co-founder of Haystack.

These jobs will require more than just word processing and spreadsheet skills, so you may need some specialist training, he says: 'I'd recommend looking into local coding academies and boot camps such as CodeClan in Scotland and Code Nation in Manchester which offer training and teaching, often partnering with organisations to help their graduates move into new roles.

'If you're looking to upskill or brush up on your tech skills, there's a whole host of online resources to tap into. A few of my favourites are Udemy, Treehouse, Wes Bos and Codecademy.'

5. Be flexible

'Adaptability is perhaps the most important skill in times of crisis,' Harvey Morton, a 23-year-old entrepreneur and founder of Harvey Morton Digital.

'It's easier to get a job when you've already got a job. It's also easier to stay resilient and mentally healthy when you know how you're going to pay the rent this month. So while I don't advocate applying for absolutely anything, keep an open mind and consider applying for a job that would be "fine for now" rather than limiting yourself only to "dream jobs".'

6. Look into volunteering

'If you've been out of work for a while or are a younger applicant who might not have any workplace experience, consider volunteering as a way to fill those gaps on your CV,' says McQueen, and there are lots of charities looking for people to help out with all kinds of projects, both in person and working remotely.

'Not only can you do good deeds and really make a difference to society, but you can also gain plenty of useful skills that can apply to any other work environment. Taking the time to volunteer also highlights to an employer your drive and work ethic, which again is welcome in any team.'

15 July 2021

Tips to improve your employability

Job hunting can be a frustrating and sometimes disappointing exercise. If you've received a few knock backs and are feeling a bit disheartened, take a step back for a moment and consider how you can boost your employability and improve your chances of finding a great job.

Sometimes a simple change to the way you approach your job search can make a world of difference, so here are some of our top tips on how to boost your employability.

1. Research your chosen career path

Finding out everything you can about your chosen career path will greatly help your job search. Knowing what to expect from your future role will help you to tailor your CV and application to meet the requirements of the job. Researching will also help you to understand exactly what your future job would consist of and help you to decide whether it is truly right for you.

2. Be enthusiastic

Take your job search seriously and show the employer that you are keen, enthusiastic and serious about your application. If you act like you don't really care about the future you will put yourself at a disadvantage if the employer notices your lack of enthusiasm. Don't let previous knock backs damage your enthusiasm and treat each application and each job interview as a new opportunity.

3. Get help, advice & guidance

At Steps To Work we offer free, unbiased help, advice and guidance to those looking for a job. We can help with all areas of employability whether you need help updating your CV or you simply need some advice on how to improve your motivation and perform better in interviews. Our trained information, advice and guidance officers know their stuff and will be able to identify issues in your job search approach and help you to boost your employability and improve your chances of finding a job.

4. Practise your interview technique

If you have been getting to the interview stage then you're obviously doing something right in your application to impress the employer enough to want to meet you face to face. But if you find that you're falling at the last hurdle and not making it through the interview stage it may be time to practise your interview technique. At Steps to Work we can offer mock interviews and one to one sessions to help you improve your technique and prepare answers to those tricky interview questions so that you're no longer left lost for words when it comes to the real thing.

5. Don't tell porkies

Never tell lies, bend the truth or exaggerate when it comes to applying for a job. You will undoubtedly get found out if you do tell a lie and this won't look good to your employer. If, for example, they're asking for a C in GCSE Maths and you actually got an E don't lie; no matter how unlikely it seems that the employer will ever find out it is always better to tell the truth. If you're asked a question in the interview that you don't know the answer to it's always best to admit that you don't know rather than ramble and try to guess the answer. Consider saying something like 'I don't know however that is an area in which I am keen to develop my skills and understanding and would like the opportunity to learn'. Your honesty and your willingness to learn will look good to an employer.

If you've been job hunting for a while and had no luck, consider getting some help and advice from a professional. These days there are lots of resources out there for job seekers, many of which are free, and you shouldn't be afraid to seek advice.

While it's tempting to stick with what you know and are comfortable with it is important to be flexible in your approach. If your current approach isn't working for you it is important to try different things and be open to advice and guidance; you might just find it's the best thing you ever did!

6 ways recent college graduates can enhance their online job search

An article from The Conversation.

By Jason Eckert, Executive Director of Career Services, University of Dayton

THE CONVERSATION

When recent or soon-to-be college graduates begin to seek employment, many inevitably turn to job-search and networking platforms on the internet.

The platforms include some that are college-based – such as Handshake, Symplicity GradLeaders and 12twenty – as well as networking platforms like LinkedIn and PeopleGrove. With COVID-19 having moved job searches more and more into the virtual realm, these platforms are playing an increasingly crucial role in the quest for employment.

From my vantage point as a veteran college-based career services counsellor, I have also observed that many students and recent graduates don't make the most of what these platforms have to offer.

With that in mind – and in light of reports of bleak employment prospects for new college graduates – here are six tips for recent or soon-to-be college graduates who hope to make the most of their virtual job searches.

1. Use multiple platforms

Start with the platform that has a partnership with your college. The reason is because campus-based platforms, such as Symplicity or Handshake, often list jobs that are not available on other sites.

At the same time, I recommend that college students set up profiles with one or more of the 'big board' employment job posting sites, such as Indeed, CareerBuilder, SimplyHired, ZipRecruiter or Glassdoor. Among other things, these sites allow job seekers to create job search agents that push email notifications whenever new jobs that match search criteria are posted.

2. Apply frequently

Students who are new to the job search may not be applying for enough positions. I've recently worked with several students who have become discouraged when they applied to a few jobs and didn't get the response they wanted.

While the number of positions a college job seeker should apply to will vary by industry, I suggest that an applicant should apply to at least two or three positions a day.

The reason I say this is because employment experts, such as Biron Clark, founder of CareerSidekick.com, estimate that only 2%-3% of employment applications result in an interview. For that reason alone, job seekers have to step up their search and networking efforts in order to increase their odds.

3. Set small daily goals

Real and perceived economic challenges created by the pandemic have led to a great deal of anxiety for job seekers. Studies have shown that extended periods of unemployment – and the risk of unemployment and underemployment – can be distressing.

Many college students with whom I have worked have expressed feelings of anxiety and being overwhelmed about their employment prospects. Some have even stopped searching for a job altogether.

To guard against giving up, I recommend that college students and recent graduates focus on small steps and daily goals. In addition to applying to a few positions a day, these goals can include conducting research regarding possible careers or networking with at least one person daily.

4. Track your progress

Create a spreadsheet to keep track of your job applications.

I believe a spreadsheet can be a motivational tool to ensure daily job hunt activity. I've even created a sample spreadsheet that I share with the students and alumni with whom I work. The columns on my sample spreadsheet include categories such as 'Date of Application,' 'Date of Screening Interview,' 'Thank You Note Sent?' and 'Salary Offer.'

A more sophisticated spreadsheet might include columns for when the time comes to choose between offers, such as length of commute or average rent in the city where the job is located.

5. Tap into alumni networks

Surveys indicate that up to 80% of people secure employment opportunities through networking and personal connections. For that reason, connections with alumni and others with ties to a particular school can be the key to a successful job search.

Many colleges and universities have programs to help students and alumni make connections. Some of these are closed networks exclusively for current students and verified alumni, often through service providers such as PeopleGrove and Graduway. Others are through LinkedIn, including specific university-affiliated LinkedIn groups and the popular LinkedIn Alumni Tool. This tool allows job seekers to research and connect with alumni from their alma mater based on search criteria that include geographic location, current employer, job function and industry, academic major and skills.

While networking strategies can feel like a lot of work, they are proven. Sometimes the progress is incremental. For instance, networking can lead to informational interviews, which are opportunities for job seekers to get insights from someone already working in a field or at a company of interest.

I have seen the power of networking and these informational interviews firsthand. A 2020 graduate from the school where I work landed a position as an area manager with a major logistics company in Orlando after we connected him with an alum who works for the same organization. The alum offered him an informational interview and made an internal employee referral. A formal job interview and, ultimately, a job offer soon followed.

6. Take advantage of career services

As a career services professional, I would be remiss if I failed to point out that almost every college and university has some sort of career centre to help students find jobs. The vast majority offer services to alumni for life for free or for a small fee.

Evidence shows that visits to these centres are worthwhile. According to a 2016 Gallup poll, college graduates who use their college career centre are more likely to obtain full-time employment – 67%, compared with 59% for graduates who did not visit career services.

16 April 2021

How to write a CV

Create a CV that stands out and gets you an interview.

Why you need a CV

A CV is a short, written summary of your skills, achievements and experience which relate to a role you want. You use it in the first stage of applying for jobs. Employers often ask for a CV instead of an application form but sometimes you'll need both.

It's your first chance to promote yourself to an employer. A good CV will get you to an interview.

Use it to apply for advertised jobs, or to introduce yourself to employers you'd like to work for. They may have vacancies that aren't advertised.

Start your CV

Start with the job advert for the role you're applying for, so you can refer to the:

♦ job description

♦ person specification

♦ company details

Think about how your skills and experience match what the employer is looking for and gather the information you'll need, including:

♦ your qualifications

♦ your past jobs and volunteering experience

♦ your past employers' details

♦ evidence of any training courses you've completed

You should tailor your CV to suit the job description and the company. If the job you're applying for does not have a job description, you can look at our job profiles to understand the skills you'll need and the typical things you'll do in that job.

Layout

There are different CV styles, so use the one which best matches the role and the stage you're at in your life or career.

♦ traditional CV or chronological CV - lists your work and education history, starting with the most recent

♦ skills based or targeted CV - focuses on your job-related skills and personal qualities

♦ technical CV - used in professions like IT and engineering, it highlights the skills you have that are important in your industry

♦ creative CV - used in creative and digital arts and can link to an online portfolio, contain video or infographics, or include digital tools that make you stand out from the crowd

♦ academic CV - generally longer than a traditional or skills-based CV and often used for teaching and research careers

Your finished CV should be no more than 2 sides of A4 unless it's an academic CV.

What to include in your CV

There are some things that you need to put in your CV. You can change the order of these to suit your situation and the type of CV layout you want to use.

Contact details

You'll need to provide details of how employers can get in touch with you if they want to offer you an interview.

You should only include your:

♦ name at the top of the page - no need to add 'CV' or 'curriculum vitae'

♦ phone number which employers can reach you on during the working day

♦ email address - always use a professional sounding email address

You can also provide a link to your professional networking profile, like LinkedIn.

Do not include your:

♦ age

♦ date of birth

♦ marital status

♦ nationality

Personal profile

This is a few short lines that sum up who you are and what you hope to do. It should go just under your name and contact details.

Think about the job you want and what the employer is looking for. Make your profile sound like you're the right person for the job.

Education history

You can add this section after your personal profile if you're early on in your career, or if you don't have much work experience. Whatever order you choose, you'll need to include the:

♦ names of your qualifications

♦ school, college or university where you studied

♦ dates you attended

If you're older and have had a number of jobs, you might want to change the order and show your work history and skills first.

Work history

Include placements, volunteering and any paid jobs you've had. You should list these with the most recent first, and include:

♦ the employer details

♦ the job title

♦ the dates you worked there

♦ what you did (usually 2 to 3 lines)

Use active words to highlight your strengths and skills, to describe things you've done like:

♦ organised

♦ created

- ◆ built

- ◆ managed

- ◆ planned

Give positive examples of your achievements rather than just listing responsibilities.

If you've had a lot of jobs, you can use a skills-based CV to group them.

Gaps in your CV

A skills-based CV is useful when you have gaps in your work history. Give examples of skills you've developed during the times you were out of work and how you got them.

If you need help explaining times when you were not able to work, you can get advice from organisations like:

- ◆ Rethink if you've been affected by mental illness

- ◆ Carers UK for returning to work after caring

- ◆ Nacro for support if you have a criminal record

If you're applying for your first job, you can focus on skills you've learned through:

- ◆ projects

- ◆ part-time work

- ◆ work experience

- ◆ internships and placements

- ◆ volunteering

Hobbies, interests or achievements

Try to show the skills you have through your hobbies and interests. Focus on examples that show you have relevant skills for the job.

This section of a CV is useful if you do not have much work experience.

References

You can leave out the details of your references at this point, or mention that 'references are available on request'. The recruiter will ask for these when you get through to the next stage.

CV tips

Employers get lots of CVs to look at and have to decide quickly who they are going to interview. Here are some tips to make your CV stand out for all the right reasons.

When writing your CV remember to:

- ◆ research the company and the job before you start

- ◆ choose a CV style that fits your situation or one that employers in that sector prefer

- ◆ use a clear font like Arial, Times New Roman or Calibri, size 11 or bigger. Always use the same style throughout

- ◆ use headings, bullet points and spacing to break information up to make it easier to read

- ◆ keep it to 2 sides of A4

- ◆ be clear and to the point

- ◆ match the words you use to the keywords in the job description

- ◆ get someone else to read it, and double check your spelling and grammar

- ◆ save a backup copy and convert it to PDF format for emailing

- ◆ always send a cover letter with your CV

www.nationalcareers.service.gov.uk

How to make your cover letter stand out?

By Daniela Mcvicker

Imagine reading this fifty times a day.

'Dear Sir or Madam,

I'm writing to apply for the position of the assistant manager with your company.'

This is what recruiters and hiring managers do constantly.

When a good position gets posted online, it receives about 200+ resumes and cover letters from job seekers. To find the best candidates, the employer needs to go through all of them.

As you can imagine, a traditional cover letter that begins with *'Dear Sir or Madam…'* isn't a good way to stand out. The way you write your cover letter is as important as the content, so you need to know how to make it more memorable.

In this article, you'll find the best tips on how to make that happen.

Writing a memorable cover letter: the essentials

Let me start by walking you through the essentials of writing a cover letter. These are the simplest but critical requirements to meet.

So, please keep in mind these points before writing:

- **keep it short.** The ideal length of a cover letter is between 250 and 300 words. This is equivalent to one page of text, so plan your ideas and outline accordingly

- **state the position clearly.** Some people who are new to the job-seeking process (especially graduates), use cover letter templates. Often, they write a generic introduction without the name of the position they applied to. So, please ensure that your recruiters don't have to guess about anything

- **find out the name of the person you are sending the cover letter to.** Addressing the reader by name will add a personal touch, and help your cover letter to stand out

- **include some numbers.** It's important to support your accomplishments with some specific, useful data. That's why try to find some numbers before sitting down to write your cover letter

- **look for cover letter mentions in the job description.** Some employers make sure that the applicants read job descriptions by making special requests

In this job description, for example, the recruiter wants applicants to specify salary requirements.

'Please submit a resume and cover letter with salary requirements.'

Requests like these can be as simple as writing *'I've read the description at the beginning of the cover letter,'* but they're important for the employer. So, pay attention to descriptions and address them accordingly.

Doing this will help you to make your cover letter short enough to read quickly. Also, you'll avoid most of the silly mistakes that many graduates make.

Now that we're feeling more confident, let's talk about specifics.

5 tips how to write a cover letter that stands out

In this section, you'll find tips on how to write a truly unique cover letter that gives you a great chance to stand out from the rest.

1. Say no to academic writing style

As a fresh graduate, you're used to writing in the academic style. All those essays and research papers you've written throughout the student years had to follow a bunch of strict styles and tone requirements to get a nice grade.

For a recruiter, though, reading a cover letter in an academic style would be a weird experience. For one, they'll know how it feels to a university professor who's reading an essay.

While you certainly should keep the tone of writing professional, there's no need to use complex academic-style words. The only thing they'll do is make the cover letter more complicated.

Besides, many employers use natural, simple language to write job descriptions.

Try to mirror their style in your cover letter. In the above example, reading the text feels like having a conversation with the recruiter.

In this particular case, writing the cover letter in a similar tone and style would be a good idea.

2. Start by explaining why you're passionate about the job

This is one excellent way to make your cover letter stand out.

Start with the name of the person you're sending the cover letter to (if you know their name), or a simple 'Hello,' and consider writing something like this.

Example 1

'I've been writing a personal blog since 2012, so it felt right to turn this passion into a career.'

Example 2

'After trying five career assessments, having one-on-one career coaching sessions, and reading tons of advice on career planning, I've come to the conclusion that I'm really good at one thing: writing web content.'

Example 3

'Among my friends, I'm known as the most empathetic one who can always listen and give advice. That's true: I like to help people and have a knack for communication. This is why I think I would be a great fit for the position of customer support specialist.'

An introduction like this would be a nice change among those 'Dear Sir or Madam' ones. The recruiter is more likely to be genuinely interested in reading more.

3. Tell them you have the skills

The recruiter reading your cover letter is likely to have a list of skills and competencies by which they judge the applications. That's why you should mention them in the first part of your letter.

Before writing your letter, choose at least five skills and five competencies that are relevant to the role you're applying for. Here's how you can mention them.

'As a candidate, here's how I can help your company:

Superb time management skills. In my internship at [company name], I've managed to complete [example KPIs] within [timeframe] because of the excellent time management skills.

Fast learning skills. I'm a passionate learner, eager to obtain new skills needed to find new growth ideas. Your position requires the best candidate to be willing to learn many new marketing techniques fast, so this is not a problem for me.'

Be sure to mention how a skill of competence is relevant to the position.

4. Mention your degree and school

Now that you've grabbed their attention with how passionate you are about that job, it's time to give them more reasons to consider you.

This means mentioning the info about your degree, college, internships, and other experiences.

Here's an example.

'As a recent graduate of [University name], I have a significant background in copywriting. As a journalist major, I took part in multiple internships at marketing agencies, including a junior copywriter at [Company Name].'

As you can see, this example briefly mentions the degree and goes straight to the experience. This is a deliberate tactic because the cover letter must highlight the experience that the employer is looking for.

Pro Tip!

'Feel free to bold the most important words in the experience section,' says Aaron Kielce, a writing consultant at Trustmypaper. 'It'll help to draw the attention of the reader and allow them to get the essential info even without reading the entire document.'

5. Describe an impressive achievement

The fact that you had multiple internships is great. But remember that there might be 200+ people like you with a similar experience.

Since we're here to help you stand out from the crowd, you need to describe the most important accomplishments you had during your studies or internships.

Here are a couple of examples for inspiration.

'After my second month as an intern at [Company name], I was promoted to an assistant. That position had me perform sales analytics and compile weekly reports. This means I'm ready for a challenge, so the position of the sales manager might be it.'

'I've completed my first internship with a college football team while I was a sophomore. After the third year, I was hired as a second assistant to the offensive coordinator. Within just three weeks, I was promoted to the first assistant.'

While any impressive accomplishments are great, be sure to mention those related to the position you're applying for. Mentioning the skills that led you to that achievement would also be a big plus.

How to structure a cover letter

Employers will be interested to see how you structure your cover letter. They will be looking to see how you format the document and present information.

Whilst the general structure of your cover letters will be more or less the same, it's important to tailor your cover letter for every role.

Within the first paragraph, outline:

♦ Why you are writing

♦ The job you are applying for

♦ Where you saw the job advert

In the second paragraph, outline:

♦ What you can bring to the role specifically

♦ Why you are applying to their particular company

Standing out isn't easy

But it's not impossible, either. Even though an average job receives 200+ applications, you can differentiate yourself from others. Writing a great cover letter is a perfect way to achieve that goal.

Once again, in this article, we didn't talk about the obvious things like listing your qualifications. They are critical but won't help you stand out. If you add the motivation and passion for the role, you'll increase the chance of impressing the person reading your cover letter.

Okay, we're done here. Good luck with your applications!

5 July 2020

How to find work experience in school

How can you find great work experience placements while you're at school? Check out our tips for school students in the UK.

By Jess Amy Dixon

Work experience is an enormously valuable part of your education. It allows you to spend time in a workplace and experience working life in a real-world setting. It looks great on your CV, allows you to hone your skills, and gives you a chance to try out a line of work to see if it's for you.

Most school students will do work experience in Year 10, or occasionally in Year 11. If you go to Sixth Form or a further education college, you might also get a chance to do additional work experience in Year 12. Most placements last one or two weeks.

There are several ways to find great work experience placements for school students. Read on for a few of our top tips to help you find the right placement for you.

Start early

Finding a great work experience placement begins with great planning. This means you need to start looking for placements well in advance of your work experience period beginning.

Your school should let you know your work experience dates in plenty of time, if you have to do your placement during a specific week (less commonly, schools will allow you to make your own arrangements as long as your placement does not conflict with important dates such as exams).

As a guide, start researching work experience opportunities at least three months in advance of when you hope to carry out your placement.

Decide what you'd like to do

Many students already know exactly what they'd like to do for their work experience. If you already have a career path in mind, you'll want to look for something related to that field. Your tutor or careers advisor should be able to help you identify possibilities based on your chosen career.

But what if you don't know what you want to do yet? First, don't panic. It's completely normal to not have your future career mapped out yet. Here are a few questions to ask yourself as you start narrowing down your options:

- What are my strengths and weaknesses?
- What subjects do I enjoy, and am I good at, at school?
- What sort of career can I imagine myself in?
- Do any of my hobbies or interests translate to possible career paths?

You can also try the UCAS Career Quiz or ask your friends, family, and teachers for their thoughts on what you'd be good at.

Find a placement through your school

Many schools have existing agreements in place with local workplaces to provide work experience for students. If yours has something like this, it's a great place to start.

Talk to your tutor or careers advisor and ask them whether the school has any such arrangements in place. It's best if you have at least a general idea of what you'd like to do at this stage.

Once you've identified a suitable placement, follow the instructions for how to apply. You may need to complete a form, send a letter, use an online application system, or provide a letter of recommendation from a teacher.

Look at large companies

Many large companies have well-established work experience schemes, both at their head offices (which tend to be located in big cities) and at their branches all over the country. So if there's a particular company that appeals to you, Google their name and the words 'work experience' to see what's available.

These schemes tend to be competitive, so take the time to make your application as good as it can possibly be. It's also a good idea to apply for more than one placement in case you receive a rejection from your first choice.

Severn Trent and McDonald's are just some of the major companies that offer work experience schemes.

Consider small and local businesses

Many smaller and local companies do not have dedicated work experience schemes, but may still be prepared to take you on for a placement. If there's an organisation in your area that appeals to you, just reach out and ask.

Start by dropping in, making a call, or sending an email to the manager to make your initial enquiry. Tell them a little bit about who you are, why you're interested in work experience at their business, and what you can bring to the table. Then ask if they'd be open to offering you a placement and if so, how you should go about formally applying.

Think outside the box

Remember that you're not limited to traditional businesses for your work experience. Many students also find placements at charities, public sector organisations, local government, the arts and cultural sector, and even schools and other educational organisations.

The most important thing is not to limit yourself. Get creative and you might find that there are far more possibilities open to you than you initially imagined.

Tips for a great application

You should approach your work experience placement in the same way you would a job application. In other words, you need to make an effort to put in the best application you can and convince the prospective employer that they need you on their team.

Here are a few tips to follow as you craft your work experience application:

♦ Always follow the instructions and never try to bypass the specified application process.

♦ Address the right person and make sure you spell their name correctly.

♦ Be positive, but be yourself.

♦ Talk about what you can offer to them.

♦ Tailor your application to each individual placement. Employers can tell if you send them something generic.

♦ Use the correct sign-off ('Yours Sincerely' if you are addressing the recipient by name, and 'Yours Truly' if you don't know their name.)

♦ Proofread your application and double-check your spelling before you send it.

♦ Always send your application well in advance of the deadline.

Good luck with finding a great placement!

16 March 2022

Interview tips

Make a good impression at a job interview, with advice on how to prepare, and how to show what you have to offer.

Why interviews are important

An interview is a chance for an employer to see if you're the right person for the job. It's also a chance for you to make sure the job and company are the right fit for you.

Where interviews take place

You may have a face-to-face interview, a phone interview, or a video interview.

Since the start of the COVID-19 pandemic, many interviews are taking place online. You're likely to use video conferencing software like Skype, Zoom or Teams.

Types of interview

There are different types of interviews which employers might use. You should prepare for the one you're attending.

One-to-one interview

Your interview may only be with one person. This is usually face-to-face, and is more common in smaller companies.

Panel interview

Some interviews are with a panel of 2 or more people. Make sure you look at all the interviewers when you're speaking with them. They may also ask you to do a presentation.

Group discussion

A group discussion is usually part of an assessment centre day with other candidates. You'll have to show you can get along with people, put your ideas forward and be respectful of others.

Types of interview questions

Employers use different types of questions when interviewing. They may tell you beforehand what type of interview it is. They may also have information on their website about their recruitment process.

Competency-based questions

The focus is on the things you can do, so you'll need to give examples to show you have the skills for the job. If you do not have examples from a work environment, you can use experiences from your personal life.

You may find out before the interview which competencies they're measuring you against.

Strengths-based questions

These explore what you enjoy doing or do well. For example, your practical or team working skills, or how you work under pressure.

Technical questions

The employer may test your job-related knowledge and understanding of work processes. This is common for jobs in:

- science
- IT
- engineering
- finance
- law

Situational judgement questions

Employers may ask how you would react in typical work situations. This is to check things like your ability to solve problems, make decisions or work with others.

Values-based questions

Value-based questions identify whether you share the organisation's values and understand their culture. This is common for health and care jobs, particularly in the NHS.

Motivational questions

These help an employer to see what drives you and to make sure you'll fit in with their company.

Learn what other people say it's like to work at the company or in a similar job. People post their interview experiences on websites like The Student Room and Glassdoor.

You could also talk to people you know who work at the company or are in similar jobs.

Prepare

Choose a date and time that works for you so you can be ready for the interview and be at your best on the day.

To help make sure you're prepared:

- read the job description and person specification carefully. Be clear on the skills and qualities the employer is looking for
- check the company website to find out more about its products or services and their plans for the future
- go over your CV or application form and think about things the employer may ask you about
- prepare some examples that show you have the right skills, personal qualities and experience. Use the STAR method
- practise your timings on presentations and keep a back-up copy
- ask someone you trust to help you practise answering questions
- think of 2 or 3 questions of your own that you can ask at the end of your interview, to show you're enthusiastic about the job
- pick out something suitable and comfortable to wear
- check what time you need to arrive and the name of the person you need to see
- make sure that you know how to get to where the interview is being held. Work out your public transport route or where you can park. Plan to arrive 5 to 10 minutes before the interview starts
- make sure you know who to call in case you're late for any reason

If you have a disability you may need adjustments to make the interview accessible. You can get advice from Scope on how to ask for adjustments at an interview.

Arriving

Before you go into the interview:

♦ turn off your phone

♦ use breathing techniques to calm yourself - try to remember, a few nerves are normal

♦ smile and greet your interviewer with confidence

♦ ask for some water if you need it

The interview

In the interview, remember to:

♦ be polite and use the right language and tone for a formal situation

♦ listen to the questions and think before you begin your answers

♦ ask the interviewer to repeat or explain further if you do not understand a question

♦ be positive about your experiences. If you've faced difficult situations, show what you learned from them

♦ be honest and assertive

♦ ask a couple of questions when you're given the opportunity. Choose questions that make you sound keen. For example, 'What opportunities are there for training with the company?' It's best not to ask about pay or holidays at this stage

At the end of the interview, thank the employer for their time. Tell them you're looking forward to hearing from them.

After the interview

When you leave the interview, try to reflect on some of the harder questions you were asked - this can help you to prepare for future interviews.

Accepting a job

If you're offered the job, let the company know in good time whether you want to accept the offer. You can also agree when you'll start and find out what you'll need to do on your first day.

Turning down a job

If you decide not to accept the job, turn it down but be polite. You may want to work for them in the future.

If you're not successful

If the employer does not offer you the job:

♦ try to be positive - this is a chance to learn from your experience and build your resilience

♦ ask for feedback on your interview

♦ think about the things that did not go so well and what you could do to improve next time

♦ get some interview practice. Ask friends, family, colleagues or a careers adviser to help

10 best job interview tips

Once you've written a stand-out cover letter and nabbed yourself a job interview, the application process starts to feel very real. But don't worry – we're here to make sure you blow them away.

By Jake Butler

When you think of job interviews, you might be conjuring up thoughts of a particularly painful episode of The Apprentice. But, they really aren't all that bad (we promise).

Remember that your interviewers are hoping to find their ideal candidate, so they want you to do well – it makes zero sense for them to try to trip you up. A little bit of plan and prep is all you need to walk into your interview brimming with confidence, and the rest will fall into place.

Although your CV is crucial in building a picture of you and your experience, an interview is your chance to really sell yourself and wow your potential future employer. Read on for some top tips for interviews for students to help you secure that dream job.

How to succeed in a job interview

Follow these tips on what to do before, during and after job interviews to really impress employers:

1. Research the role, company and industry

Turning up for an interview without being armed with interesting things to say about the company or sector as well as yourself and your work experience is the easiest mistake to make.

Do some research by looking carefully at the company website, following their social media accounts and googling them to see if you can find any press coverage or even a company blog.

A pro tip is to set up a Google Alert for the company name so that you get any relevant news about them straight to your inbox.

Why is it important to prepare for an interview? If you're really well informed, you'll not only impress your interviewers, but it'll also give you a better picture of what you're potentially signing yourself up to.

It's also a good idea to research the wider sector so you can show awareness of any hot topics and who the company's competitors are.

Most employers say that it's obvious when a candidate hasn't prepared adequately, so the knowledge you gather on these subjects will suggest you have a genuine interest and that you're willing to go the extra mile.

It'll also make conversation flow easily and reduce the chances of any awkward silent moments.

2. List your skills that are most relevant to the role

Now you've done your research on the company and sector, it's time to start thinking about which aspects of your skillset and experience are directly relevant to the company and the job role.

Read through the job description, pull out the most important parts and make a list.

Next to each point, write down any parts of your own CV or things about yourself that come to mind that you know demonstrate you have something to offer that directly relates to each point.

It's pretty much guaranteed that the interviewer will use the job description to direct the conversation, so preparing in this way will give you go-to responses when you hear the key buzzwords.

Prepare these in advance and read them over and over so that when it comes to interview questions about a certain competency, then an example will pop straight to mind. This can also help prevent you from repeating yourself with the same examples.

For a bit of extra help, check out the skills that employers want the most.

3. Prepare your own questions

The questions you ask at the end of an interview are so important, both to give you the opportunity to find out more, and also to show the interviewer that you're engaged, inquisitive and keen to learn about the role and company.

Being able to ask interesting questions is as important as answering them, so take the time to prepare a few.

Just make sure you don't ask anything that's already been covered in the interview, or it'll seem like you weren't listening.

Best questions to ask in an interview

It's best to keep your questions as tailored to the job role and company as you can, but here are some examples if you're struggling to think of anything:

♦ 'What are the most important qualities for the ideal candidate for this role?' – This shows that you (like your interviewer) are interested in knowing if you're right for the job and will also give you an idea of whether you've covered everything they were expecting from you.

♦ 'How does the company help employees with career progression?' – From this question, the interviewer will see you're ambitious and it gives them an opportunity to 'sell' the company to you.

♦ 'How is the team structured and who would I be reporting to?' – The interviewer will be looking to see if you would fit into the team. Showing an interest in the people you'd be working with and for will make a good impression.

4. Wake up early on the morning of your interview

An obvious one we know, but we'll say it anyway: get up extra early on the morning of your interview.

If you have time, go for a run or to the gym to wake yourself up and get those endorphins going – this will calm the jitters and give you a confidence boost.

You should also aim to give yourself enough time to sit down for breakfast before leaving for the interview. We know that when you're nervous before an interview, it can sometimes be hard to eat, but try to have as good a meal as you can.

You don't have to go all out with a full English, but try to eat a bit of brain food beforehand – we recommend a bowl of cereal, some fruit, toast and a cup of tea or coffee. You could also take an apple with you to fight those mid-morning hunger pains.

Before you head in for your interview, have a chat with a friend or family member about something other than the interview to loosen yourself up and get into the swing of things. Nothing like a natter about EastEnders to take your mind off your nerves.

5. Plan out the interview day in advance

Planning everything in advance will put your mind at ease and ensure nothing goes wrong on the day.

Choose what you're going to wear (wearing smart work clothes but nothing too formal will give a good impression) at least a couple of days before the interview.

This will cancel out any potentially disastrous moments where you realise your lucky shirt has a massive blob of ketchup down the front and you need to wash it last minute in a blind panic.

We'd recommend also carefully planning out your journey to the interview and even testing out the route if you have time. It's always better to turn up early (at least five minutes early!) than it is to be late, so make sure to leave some extra time.

It's also best to pack your bag with everything you'll need the night before.

What to bring to a job interview

♦ A few copies of your CV

♦ Business cards (if you have any)

- ♦ Your passport
- ♦ A portfolio of your work (if you have or need one)
- ♦ A pen and paper to take any notes
- ♦ Any questions you prepared.

6. Try to stay calm during your interview

Try to calm your nerves on the day by not obsessing about what's ahead too much. After all that great prep you've been doing over the last few days, there's not much more you'll achieve by thinking about it incessantly – that will only make you more nervous.

Always remember that it's normal for you to get a bit nervous and most employers will expect you to be!

What to do if you feel nervous in a job interview

- ♦ Smile and give a firm handshake when greeting your interviewer – there's nothing worse than a limp handshake.

- ♦ Ask a short icebreaker question when you first arrive to get things going on an informal level, like 'How's your day going?'.

- ♦ Think about your posture and make sure when you take a seat you're sitting up straight and not fidgeting. Hand gestures can be good for emphasis when you're talking, but don't overdo it. Try not to sit completely rigid either, or you'll look (and feel!) uncomfortable and more nervous.

- ♦ Remember that you're talking to a professional and be mindful of your vocabulary. If you start to go on a tangent, stop yourself ASAP and try not to say things such as 'erm' too much – take a second and breathe.

- ♦ Compose yourself when answering questions and take time to think. You can think back to the notes you've written and then give the best answer that you can. Much better than rushing straight into it.

7. Answer opening interview questions concisely

The interview will likely start with a few general opening questions, and as easy as these questions might seem, they can throw you off if you haven't prepared adequately.

Usually, job interviews will start with a generic opening question like 'could you tell me a bit about yourself?'. When asked this, try not to launch into your entire life story, as this isn't what they're asking.

What this question really means is 'tell us in a few sentences why you're a relevant candidate to this company and role', so things like your degree, uni and what has made you decide to go for a career in this area will suffice.

You can also mention things like where you're from if you're applying somewhere away from home, but keep it brief.

Although these are just warm-up questions, don't take them too informally as first impressions are incredibly important.

8. Use examples to answer competency-based questions

You can expect that the follow-on questions from the opening ones will then draw on examples and experiences to test your key competencies. This is where your preparation will really start to pay off.

Many employers report that a lot of candidates lack a wide range of examples and are too vague in interviews.

Interviewers don't want to hear about what you've been doing at university for every question, so if you want to stand out in a job interview, think outside the box by using examples from your life outside of education and at previous part-time jobs.

9. Handle difficult interview questions confidently

If a difficult question comes up, there's no hard and fast rule for handling it. It's easier said than done in a high-pressure interview environment, but try to stay calm and just answer the question as best you can.

Here are some top tips on how to answer difficult interview questions:

- ♦ Answer the question directly (avoid waffling and going off on a tangent)

- ♦ Give clear and tangible examples when you can

- ♦ Show you've thought about how your current skills are relevant/transferable to the job

- ♦ As well as talking about your strengths, highlight that you're keen to continue learning and improving in a new role.

10. Thank interviewers in a follow-up email

Once the interview is over, there are still a few things you can do to give yourself an advantage over other candidates in securing the job. A follow-up email to thank the employer for seeing you and giving you their time is always a good idea and will keep you at the forefront of their minds.

If you haven't heard back from them in two weeks or more, send an email or phone them up to ask for feedback.

Even if you didn't get the job this time, remember that every interview is a learning experience and you'll only get better and better at it each time you walk into an interview.

The last thing to say is simply... good luck!

2 December 2021

Youth unemployment statistics

An extract.

By Andrew Powell, Brigid Francis-Devine & Harriet Clark

Unemployment and education status

162,000 unemployed young people were in full-time education (33% of all unemployed young people) in November 2021-January 2022, similar to the previous quarter and a fall of 25,000 from the year before. Excluding those in full-time education, 295,000 people aged 16-24 were unemployed. This is similar to the previous quarter, and a fall of 104,000 from the year before.

The unemployment rate for 16-24 year olds in full-time education was 14.0%, down from 19.5% a year before. It was 9.9% for those not in full-time education, down from 12.1% a year before.

Unemployment by age

358,000 18-24 year olds were unemployed in November 2021-January 2022, while 1.65 million were economically

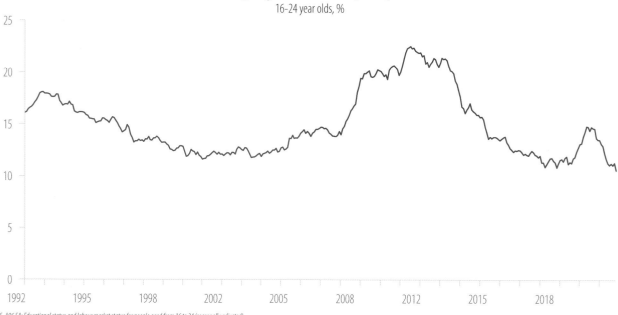

Youth unemployment rate, UK, 1992-2022
16-24 year olds, %

Source: ONS, A06 SA: Educational status and labour market status for people aged from 16 to 24 (seasonally adjusted)

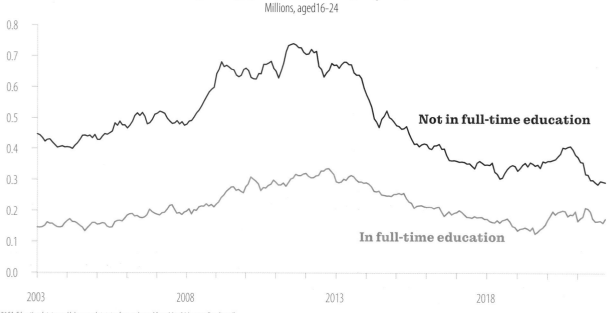

Number of young people unemployed, 2003-2022
Millions, aged 16-24

Source: ONS, A06 SA: Educational status and labour market status for people aged from 16 to 24 (seasonally adjusted)

Youth unemployment rates in OECD countries

October-December 2021

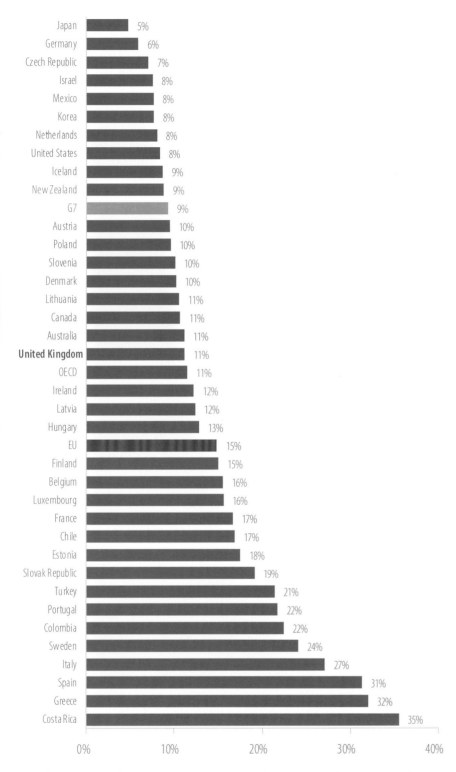

Japan	5%
Germany	6%
Czech Republic	7%
Israel	8%
Mexico	8%
Korea	8%
Netherlands	8%
United States	8%
Iceland	9%
New Zealand	9%
G7	9%
Austria	10%
Poland	10%
Slovenia	10%
Denmark	10%
Lithuania	11%
Canada	11%
Australia	11%
United Kingdom	11%
OECD	11%
Ireland	12%
Latvia	12%
Hungary	13%
EU	15%
Finland	15%
Belgium	16%
Luxembourg	16%
France	17%
Chile	17%
Estonia	18%
Slovak Republic	19%
Turkey	21%
Portugal	22%
Colombia	22%
Sweden	24%
Italy	27%
Spain	31%
Greece	32%
Costa Rica	35%

Notes: Seasonally adjusted. Rate refers to the percentage of economically active young people aged 15-24 who are unemployed (16-24 year olds in UK, the US, Iceland, Norway and Spain).
Source: OECD, Short-term labour statistics, Data extracted on 12 April 2022

inactive and 3.33 million were in work. The unemployment rate for people aged 18-24 was 9.7%, down from 13.5% a year before.

99,000 16-17 year olds were unemployed, while 1.01 million were economically inactive and 350,000 were in work.

Long term youth unemployment

89,000 people aged 16-24 had been unemployed for over 12 months in November 2021-January 2022, which was 19.5% of unemployed 16-24 year olds. This is up from 18.9% in the previous quarter.

22% of all people who had been unemployed for over 12 months were 16-24 year olds.

Men and women

265,000 men aged 16-24 were unemployed in November 2021-January 2022, an increase of 10,000 from the previous quarter and a decrease of 72,000 from the previous year. The unemployment rate for men of this age was 12.6%, down from 16.4% a year before.

192,000 women aged 16-24 were unemployed, down 11,000 from the previous quarter and down 58,000 on the previous year. The unemployment rate for women aged 16-24 was 9.5%, compared to 12.7% a year before.

17 May 2022

www.parliament.uk

Youth unemployment

The youth unemployment landscape in the UK remains a growing problem for UK employers, educators and our young people.

- Youth unemployment has been an escalating problem in the UK since 2005, with the most recent rises directly attributable to issues of the economy

- Persistent youth unemployment has been embedded in our system over decades

- Unemployment while young is linked to long-term reductions in wages, increased chances of subsequent periods of unemployment, and poorer health outcomes.

- High levels of youth unemployment also have wider social and economic costs. The cost of youth unemployment over the next decade has been estimated at £28 billion

- 'With youth unemployment nearing 1 million, supporting young people into jobs - and sustainable jobs in particular - must be a foremost priority if the UK is to avoid a lost generation.'

- UK businesses tell us they struggle to recruit young, work-ready staff

- A generation of young people lost to unemployment means an inadequate talent pool for the needs of our businesses as the economy recovers

What causes youth unemployment?

As mentioned youth unemployment has been growing since 2005 so the recession and economy bear only some of the blame for high youth unemployment levels.

Other causes such as those listed below have been cited in reports such as; Youth Unemployment: cyclical and structural concerns (CPS), Youth unemployment: the crisis we cannot afford (ACEVO), The Youth Unemployment Challenge (UKCES) to name a few.

Why do we care?

The threat of a 'lost generation' for some is quite real although according to Prof. Paul Gregg this is an exaggerated term, what we do know is that there are significant consequences.

Experiencing unemployment in youth can lead to emotional problems and can also reduce a person's life long earning/career potential, it creates further inequalities particularly between communities, and the financial costs of supporting unemployment; welfare and medical support reach into billions.

Then consider the cost to business and to the prosperity of the UK, imagine trying to recruit from a large pool of applicants with little or no work experience, where will the next generation of leaders and innovators come from? To compete in the ever changing world economy we need to have a bright, educated and skilled workforce.

Finally with nearly 1 million young people unemployed, that is approximately 1 in 5 young people, it is likely that we will all know someone in our network who will be affected by this problem, not least those still in education yet to try to gain employment.

Can youth unemployment be fixed?

Yes, we believe so. Already there are thousands of brilliant youth engagement activities and initiatives happening

What causes youth unemployment?

Lack of jobs	Gaps between education and employment
Young people lack skills needed for work	Employers prefer to work with experienced staff
Credentialism	Young people's expectations
Lack of qualifications or appropriate qualifications	Lack of accurate and engaging careers information
Rise in retirement age	Employment legislation
Recruitment Methods	Employers perceptions of young people
Poor vocational options	Lack of quality vocational pathways
Welfare	Workfare

across the UK. 1 in 4 employers are very engaged with youth activities from talking in schools through to taking on apprentices and employing graduates.

But there is more that can be done; we believe the solutions to youth unemployment are:

♦ Increase employer support

♦ Reduce employment legislation that creates a barrier for employers to work with young people

♦ Help employers to recognise the value of skills and behaviours as well as academic criteria

♦ Ensure education prioritises employability skills and careers learning for young people as well as quality academia

♦ Improve the quality and relevance of vocational routes and qualifications

♦ Ensure Careers Education is aligned with the needs of the economy, local labour market information and is motivating and inspirational

♦ Help young people to value work of all entry levels (raising aspirations is important but there are many jobs that then get overlooked)

♦ Create a welfare system that supports young people to find employment or training opportunities

♦ Improve the coordination of all of the youth engagement activities so that information can be shared, and so that young people will benefit from collaboration/improved signposting

So what benefits to an individual or organisation are there to supporting young people into employment?

♦ Investment now in youth employment and engagement will support the needs of a competitive and successful UK economy for years to come

♦ Companies that are seen to respond to the challenge of youth unemployment will gain a competitive edge as consumers exercise choices in favour of companies with positive social values

♦ Corporate Social Responsibility

♦ Building own talent pool & knowledge transfer from ageing workforce

♦ Young people bring creativity, innovation, flexibility, high energy and an understanding of new and emerging technologies

♦ There is evidence that by recruiting and investing in young people encourages loyalty and reduces attrition

♦ Workforce diversity

♦ Reduced cost - lower recruitment and wage costs

♦ Existing staff training and development – utilising existing staff to train, mentor, develop and support new younger staff

www.youthemployment.org.uk

Graduates face highest unemployment rate since austerity era

Department for Education survey finds young people in England hit hardest by job shortages due to pandemic.

By Rachel Hall and Richard Adams

Unemployment among recent graduates has risen to levels last seen during the austerity era, with young people worst affected by job shortages due to the pandemic, according to official data.

The unemployment rate for recent graduates in England aged 21 to 30 reached 6.3% in 2020, after it had gradually fallen over nearly a decade since a peak of 6.5% in 2012, in the middle of the coalition government's austerity drive.

'Between 2007 and 2020, employment rates have fluctuated slightly more for the young population compared with the working-age population. This might suggest that the employment of young people is disproportionately influenced by changing structural conditions in the economy,' stated the report on graduate labour market statistics published by the Department for Education.

Despite the rise in unemployment, pay rates held up for graduates who succeeded in finding a job, with graduates aged 21-64 being paid an average salary of £35,000, £9,500 more than their peers who did not go to university and an increase of £500 on 2019.

Salaries differed by industry and by gender, with men working in banking and finance making the most at £45,000, and women working in hotels and restaurants the least, at £26,500. Across all industries, men were paid more than women – including for graduates aged 30 and under, who are less likely to be affected by childcare responsibilities.

There were also disparities in employment rates among ethnic groups and people with disabilities. White graduates had the highest employment rate (86.8%) and proportion of high-skilled employment rate (67.0%), compared with 81.2% and 53.2% for black graduates. The rates for disabled graduates were 73.4% and 52%.

The figures showed an unemployment crisis facing young people who had not gone to university, with nearly one in four unemployed and not looking for work – almost double the rate for graduates.

Postgraduates have fared better than graduates during the pandemic, with a 1.8 percentage point gap in overall employment rates opening up compared with graduates. High-skilled employment rates were also 12.4 percentage points higher for postgraduates than graduates, while median earnings remained higher than for those with just an undergraduate degree at £42,000, the same level as in 2019.

Data on student loans in England also suggested that the pandemic employment market caused some graduates to be unable to make their scheduled repayments. According to figures for 2020-21 from the Student Loans Company, 201,900 fewer graduates made repayments through their salary than the previous year. Repayments in England are made only on income above £27,295.

The 2020-21 figures showed that the total amount of outstanding student loans for higher education rose to £160 billion, including £4.1 billion in interest, while repayments totalled £3 billion. The average loan balance for 2021 graduates was £45,060.

10 June 2021

Young working-class men have suffered the most from Covid job losses – apprenticeships can help

Youth unemployment increased faster between Spring and Autumn 2020 than at any point since the financial crisis in 2008.

By Saeed Atcha

Young people are often the most impacted by recessions, and they are likely to bear the deepest scars from the Covid pandemic.

The Social Mobility Commission's new report 'State of the Nation: Social mobility and the pandemic 2021' found young people were twice as likely to be working in sectors that were shut down than the rest of the workforce. Youth unemployment increased faster between Spring and Autumn 2020 than at any point since the financial crisis in 2008.

Across the entire workforce there has been a reduction in paid work of between 4 and 4.5 per cent. Young workers (aged 16-24) made up a disproportionate share of the fall in employment over the last year and were up to twice as likely than any other age group to be unemployed,

Working class men aged 16-24 especially bore the brunt of job losses – almost one in 10 lost paid work during the pandemic.

There are several worrying impacts of these trends.

Firstly, young people are likely to have lost out on valuable work experience, seen their skills deteriorate and missed out on opportunities for promotion.

This is true for those who are furloughed as well as for those in education who were promised experience as part of that course. Around 60 per cent of graduate employers cancelled some or all of their work experience and internship placements due to Covid-19.

This creates questions about who is getting the work experience that is available. Suppose sharp-elbowed young people from privileged backgrounds are securing limited work experience opportunities. In that case, it could lead to fewer opportunities for poorer young people who don't already have confidence or connections.

It's not all doom and gloom. Encouragingly, young people are hopeful. Our Social Mobility Barometer published earlier this year found young people are far more likely than their older counterparts to think it's becoming easier for people from less advantaged backgrounds to move up in British society (35 per cent of 18 to 24 year olds compared with 19 per cent of 25 to 49 year olds).

We want to give them reason to be optimistic, which is why the SMC is calling on the Government, employers and educators to put young people right at the heart of their policy decisions.

The UK Government should ensure that those from low socio-economic backgrounds get access to what should be one of the country's premier routes to better social mobility – apprenticeships.

We are also working with employers to ask them to know their workforce's socio-economic makeup, to actively widen their talent pool by working with local schools and further education colleges, and take a hands-on approach supporting their working-class employees to progress.

Young people from working-class backgrounds are equally as talented as people from more advantaged families. Those who have had to overcome the most can be the most valuable and hard-working employees or entrepreneurs.

Today we have a chance to make sure our future leaders represent the people they oversee, but we must take this opportunity of upheaval to act now.

20 July 2021

Overqualified and underemployed: a sombre snapshot of the labour market for young people

Graduates are leaving university with scant prospects, feeling let down by policy-makers and waking up to the generational divide. Carlotta Hartmann, IF Intern, investigates the labour market pressures facing young Brits today.

By Carlotta Hartmann

Graduates feeling let down

Young people across OECD countries have been disproportionately affected by the economic impacts of the COVID-19 pandemic. According to a recent article in the *Financial Times*, the percentage of unemployed under-25s rose from 11.5 in February 2020 to 12.95 in June 2021. In comparison, unemployment among those aged 25 and over increased by less, from 4.5 to 5.6 percent over the same period.

Young people have experienced a kind of wake-up call through the impacts of the pandemic, growing increasingly aware of the wealth gap between generations. This, paired with their dissatisfaction with democracy and frustration about their weak influence on politics in ageing populations, may be contributing to a radicalisation of the young, writes the FT.

Recent graduates disadvantaged in the job market

Young people in the United Kingdom face extra hurdles on the job market. Recent graduates – those who have left full-time education less than five years ago – are more likely to be working in non-graduate jobs than non-recent graduates, who are usually older and have been working for longer. The ONS defines non-graduate roles as those 'associated with tasks that do not normally require knowledge and skills developed through higher education to enable them to perform these tasks in a competent manner'.

Between 2011 and 2019, an average of 47.5 percent of recent graduates, as opposed to 34.7 percent of non-recent graduates, were working in non-graduate jobs. That recent graduates should begin in positions that require fewer qualifications is unsurprising, as non-recent graduates will have moved up the ladder to work in jobs that are considered graduate roles. However, the data shows a stark increase in the percentage of recent and non-recent graduates in non-graduate employment between 2001 and 2011 and, importantly, an increase that was more rapid for recent graduates (37 to 46 percent, as opposed to 29 to 33 percent).

From 2011 to 2019, the percentage of recent graduates in non-graduate employment fell slightly, while the number of non-recent graduates shows a slight increase. Still, there seems to be a mismatch in the job market; students are taking on loans to pay for tuition, but the job market fails to match them with jobs according to their qualifications.

Graduates working in non-graduate jobs are not only overqualified, but also replace workers who do not hold qualifications beyond A-level standard. Young people are thereby doubly disadvantaged, in that both recent graduates are working in non-graduate jobs and those without degrees struggle to find jobs.

COVID-19 unemployment hits young people

While data on young people's employment in graduate and non-graduate jobs for 2020 and 2021 is not yet available, it is clear that this group was particularly affected by unemployment during the pandemic. It is important to keep in mind that, overall, those holding a university degree are more likely to be employed than the population as a whole: the average graduate unemployment rate for Q1 2017 to Q3 2020 was 3.0 percent, while the total average unemployment rate for the same period was 4.7 percent.

Recent graduates, however, faced more difficulties finding jobs: the average unemployment rate for recent graduates was above the national average, at 6.3 percent. Young people who had recently finished their degrees were therefore more likely to be out of work than the population as a whole.

The data suggest that recent graduates and young people as a whole were particularly hard-hit by unemployment as a consequence of the COVID-19 pandemic. The unemployment rate for recent graduates peaked at 12 percent between July and September 2020.

While some increase in unemployment among recent graduates in these months is expected, with universities finishing in summer, the rate of 12 percent was the highest in three years. Graduates, even recent ones, were still better off than 16 to 24 year-olds overall: the youth unemployment rate was at 13.6 percent between July and September 2020.

Vacancies during COVID-19

Young people's difficult situation during the pandemic is evident in the decrease in vacancies, too. As Europe shut down in March 2020, many jobs were simply removed. Between March and May 2020, there were only 476,000 vacancies in the UK. Compared to the same period in 2019, this means there were 365,000 fewer jobs, a 42 percent decrease.

Three industries were particularly affected by this development: vacancies in wholesale and retail trade, accommodation and food services, and information and communications industries were at their lowest levels on record during the early months of the UK's lockdown.

According to ONS data, the former two of these are the industries in which the percentage of young people is greatest.

Recent graduates, many of whom spent their final months of university mandated to stay at home and sat their final exams online, were faced with further complications in the job market in 2020. Graduate vacancies were reduced and internships cancelled. As previously reported by IF, the data suggests that many attempted to stay in education, rather than graduating into such a precarious job market.

By now, the demand-side of the UK-job market has largely recovered from the pandemic. In May to July 2021, there were 953,000 vacancies. This puts the number of vacancies in the UK above its pre-pandemic level, raising the prospects of employment for young people now. Only vacancies in the wholesale and retail trade industry – the industry in which the percentage of young people is greatest! – remains below its pre-pandemic level.

What are the consequences?

The disproportionate economic impact of the crisis felt by young people in other OECD countries is mirrored in the United Kingdom. Even pre-pandemic, recent graduates were more likely than non-recent graduates to be working in non-graduate roles. This left them overqualified, and placed even more of a burden on young people without university degrees. As the country was locked down repeatedly to prevent the spread of Coronavirus, recent graduates, as well as young people as a whole, were more likely to face unemployment.

It is also clear that young people are ill-equipped to handle unemployment. Most have not had time to build up savings to fall back on, and certainly no regular pension funds to rely on. Even those who are in the privileged position that they can be supported by their families face the blow of not achieving hoped-for independence.

The impacts are immediate. After months of uncertainty that have taken a toll on young people's mental health, searching for jobs in such a competitive market is draining – especially when the chances are high that graduates will end up in jobs that they are overqualified for. It is no surprise that many young people have grown pessimistic about their futures.

26 August 2021

Minimum wage increase 2022: what the new UK National Living Wage is and how much it's going up

Questions remain over whether the hike will be enough to support families facing a cost of living crisis, with the energy cap rise set to come into effect.

By Jaymi McCann

The National Minimum Wage has increased for workers across the UK.

Rishi Sunak announced the change at the 2021 Budget, with the rise arriving around the time that the energy price cap increases, and households receive a council tax rebate to mitigate soaring costs.

But questions remain over whether the hike will be enough to support families facing a cost of living crisis, with the energy cap rise set to come into effect this month.

But what is the new rate? Here's everything you need to know.

What is the new minimum wage?

The National Minimum Wage and National Living Wage will rise, affecting around 2.5 million UK workers, according to the Department for Business, Energy and Industrial Strategy.

It was confirmed in the 2021 Budget that the National Living Wage will increase to £9.50 from 1 April 2022 – which equates to an extra £1,000 a year for a full-time worker.

Mr Sunak said at the time: 'This is a government that is on the side of working people. This wage boost ensures we're making work pay and keeps us on track to meet our target to end low pay by the end of this Parliament.'

The full range of increases:

♦ National Living Wage – new rate: £9.50, increase: 6.6 per cent

♦ 21-22 year old rate – new rate: £9.18, increase: 9.8 per cent

♦ 18-20 year old rate – new rate: £6.83, increase: 4.1 per cent

♦ 16-17 year old rate – new rate: £4.81, increase: 4.1 per cent

♦ Apprentice rate – new rate: £4.81, increase 11.9 per cent

♦ Accommodation offset – new rate: £8.70, increase: 4.1 per cent

As pay rates rise on Friday, workers are advised to visit checkyourpay.campaign.gov.uk to check if they're being paid correctly, and get advice if they're not.

These recommendations came from the Low Pay Commission – an independent advisory board – before being accepted by the Government and confirmed on 25 October 2021.

What has the reaction been?

Bryan Sanderson, Chair of the Low Pay Commission (LPC), welcomed the increases.

He said: 'The Business Secretary's strong support is especially welcome at this difficult time.

'Workers on the minimum wage care for our elderly and sick, harvest and deliver our food, and do a multitude of other tasks which help us all.

'They all deserve to be properly remunerated and respected as key members of our society.'

However, while higher wages are welcome, they're unlikely to make much of a dent in the face of the ongoing cost of living crisis.

Energy bills are set to rise dramatically as the price cap increases from £1,277 to £1,971 as of Friday 1 April.

Grocery costs, national insurance contributions and VAT on eating and drinking are all set to rise at the same time, meaning consumers will be out of pocket.

Jamie Mackenzie, director at employee benefits firm Sodexo Engage, said: 'According to the Trades Union Congress, energy bills are due to rise at least 14 times faster than wages this year, more than cancelling out the boost of the minimum wage hike, and in turn, leaving households financially vulnerable.

'As such, the minimum wage increase may not prove enough to shield all employees from rising prices, and employers must do their part to ease their financial pressures where they can.

'Our data found that employees can save over £1,600 from benefits alone, showing that discounts in supermarkets or online cashback and e-vouchers can go a long way in supporting a workforce that's feeling the pinch.'

Shadow chief secretary to the Treasury Bridget Phillipson said the rise was an 'underwhelming offer'.

'Much of it will be swallowed up by the Government's tax rises, Universal Credit cuts and failure to get a grip on energy bills,' the Labour MP said.

'It's clear that Labour is the only party serious about improving the prospects of working people.'

What is the real living wage?

As well as the National Living Wage, there is also an unofficial and voluntary 'real living wage'.

This is calculated by the Living Wage Foundation, a campaigning organisation, and is based directly on cost of living.

According to the foundation, the 'real' living wage is currently £9.90 an hour for workers across the UK and £11.05 in London, almost a pound above the mandatory National Living Wage.

Around 9,000 employers currently sign up to the scheme, including Google, Nationwide, Aviva and football clubs Chelsea and Everton.

1 April 2022

Employment status

In employment law a person's employment status helps determine:

♦ their rights

♦ their employer's responsibilities

A person may have a different employment status in tax law.

The main types of employment status are:

♦ worker

♦ employee

♦ self employed and contractor

♦ director

♦ office holder

Worker

A person is generally classed as a 'worker' if:

♦ they have a contract or other arrangement to do work or services personally for a reward (a contract can be written or unwritten)

♦ their reward is for money or a benefit in kind, for example the promise of a contract or future work

♦ they only have a limited right to send someone else to do the work (subcontract)

♦ their employer has to have work for them to do as long as the contract or arrangement lasts

♦ they are not doing the work as part of their own limited company in an arrangement where the 'employer' is actually a customer or client

Employment rights

Workers are entitled to certain employment rights, including:

♦ getting the National Minimum Wage

♦ protection against unlawful deductions from wages

♦ the statutory minimum level of paid holiday

♦ the statutory minimum length of rest breaks

♦ to work no more than 48 hours on average per week or to opt out of this right if they choose

♦ protection against unlawful discrimination

♦ protection for 'whistleblowers' who report wrongdoing in the workplace

♦ not to be treated less favourably if they work part-time

They may also be entitled to:

♦ Statutory Sick Pay

♦ Statutory Maternity Pay

♦ Statutory Paternity Pay

♦ Statutory Adoption Pay

♦ Shared Parental Pay

Agency workers have specific rights from the first day at work.

Workers usually are not entitled to:

♦ minimum notice periods if their employment will be ending, for example if an employer is dismissing them

♦ protection against unfair dismissal

♦ the right to request flexible working

♦ time off for emergencies

♦ Statutory Redundancy Pay

Casual or irregular work

Someone is likely to be a worker if most of these apply:

♦ they occasionally do work for a specific business

♦ the business does not have to offer them work and they do not have to accept it - they only work when they want to

♦ their contract with the business uses terms like 'casual', 'freelance', 'zero hours', 'as required' or something similar

♦ they had to agree with the business's terms and conditions to get work - either verbally or in writing

♦ they are under the supervision or control of a manager or director

♦ they cannot send someone else to do their work

♦ the business deducts tax and National Insurance contributions from their wages

♦ the business provides materials, tools or equipment they need to do the work

Employee

An employee is someone who works under an employment contract.

A person may be an employee in employment law but have a different status for tax purposes. Employers must work out each worker's status in both employment law and tax law.

Employment rights

All employees are workers, but an employee has extra employment rights and responsibilities that do not apply to workers who are not employees.

These rights include all of the rights workers have and:

♦ Statutory Sick Pay

♦ statutory maternity pay and leave (workers only get pay, not leave)

♦ statutory paternity pay and leave (workers only get pay, not leave)

♦ statutory adoption pay and leave (workers only get pay, not leave)

♦ statutory shared parental pay and leave (workers only get pay, not leave)

♦ minimum notice periods if their employment will be ending, for example if an employer is dismissing them

♦ protection against unfair dismissal

♦ the right to request flexible working

♦ time off for emergencies

♦ Statutory Redundancy Pay

Some of these rights require a minimum length of continuous employment before an employee qualifies for them. An employment contract may state how long this qualification period is.

Working out employment status for an employee

Someone who works for a business is probably an employee if most of the following are true:

♦ they're required to work regularly unless they're on leave, for example they're on holiday or on sick leave or on maternity leave

- they're required to do a minimum number of hours and expect to be paid for time worked
- a manager or supervisor is responsible for their workload, saying when a piece of work should be finished and how it should be done
- they cannot send someone else to do their work
- they get paid holiday
- they're entitled to contractual or Statutory Sick Pay and to maternity pay or to paternity pay
- they can join the business's pension scheme
- the business's disciplinary and grievance procedures apply to them
- they work at the business's premises or at an address specified by the business
- their contract sets out redundancy procedures
- the business provides the materials, tools and equipment for their work
- they only work for the business or if they do have another job, it's completely different from their work for the business
- their contract, statement of terms and conditions or offer letter (which can be described as an 'employment contract') uses terms like 'employer' and 'employee'

If most of these do not apply, you should work out if the person is self-employed.

Self-employed

A person is self-employed if they run their business for themselves and take responsibility for its success or failure.

Self-employed workers are not paid through PAYE, and they do not have the rights and responsibilities of an employee.

A worker must tell HM Revenue and Customs (HMRC) if they think they have become self-employed.

Someone can be both employed and self-employed at the same time, for example if they work for an employer during the day and run their own business in the evenings.

Employment rights

Employment law does not cover self-employed people in most cases because they are their own boss.

If a person is self-employed, they have:

- protection of their health and safety
- protection of their rights against discrimination (in some cases)
- the rights and responsibilities set out by the terms of the contract they have with their client

Working out if someone is self-employed

HMRC may regard someone as self-employed for tax purposes even if they have a different status in employment law.

Employers should check if a worker is self-employed in:

- tax law - in case the worker is exempt from the employer's PAYE scheme
- employment law - in case the worker has employee or worker rights

Checking their employment rights

If someone is self-employed, they do not have the rights and responsibilities of an employee or the rights and responsibilities of a worker.

Someone is probably self-employed if they're self-employed for tax purposes and most of the following are true:

- they put in bids or give quotes to get work
- they're not under direct supervision when working
- they submit invoices for the work they've done
- they're responsible for paying their own National Insurance and tax
- they do not get holiday or sick pay when they're not working
- they operate under a contract (sometimes known as a 'contract for services' or 'consultancy agreement') that uses terms like 'self-employed', 'consultant' or an 'independent contractor'

Zero hours contracts: advice for students

Young people are more likely to work a zero hours contract than anyone else – so what is it, and what do you need to know?

By Jess Amy Dixon

As of 2021, 917,000 people in the UK work on a zero hours contract. That's about 2.3% of the country's workforce. The 16-24 age group has consistently been the most represented demographic working this kind of contract.

But what is a zero hours contract and what does it mean for you?

What is a zero hours contract?

In a nutshell, a zero hours contract means that you are employed but that your employer does not guarantee you a minimum number of working hours each week.

Zero hours contracts appear in many different sectors but are particularly prevalent in industries such as retail, food service, leisure and hospitality, and health and social care.

Zero hours contracts are controversial, with many trade unions and other workers' rights organisations considering them unfair and exploitative. But they are a reality of the current labour market and don't look set to disappear any time soon. So what are the pros and cons and how can you make them work for you?

What are the pros and cons of a zero hours contract?

Pros

Zero hours contracts give you flexibility. For students with busy schedules and lots of demands on their time, this can be a blessing. If you're asked to work a shift that conflicts with your class schedule, you can simply refuse it.

There's also the possibility that a zero hours contract could lead to a fixed hours or permanent role, or even lay the groundwork for a full time job when you graduate. This is never a guarantee, but working a zero hours contract as a student can be a good way to get your foot in the door.

Finally, when you're a student, any work experience is a positive thing. Your zero hours contract job will enhance your skills, add to your CV, and give you something to talk about in future job interviews.

Cons

The main downside of a zero hours contract is that your income is not guaranteed. This can be very stressful, since money is often tight for students. And if you are not actually given any working hours (or are given very few), you won't enjoy those skill-enhancing and CV-building benefits we just discussed.

Zero hours contract workers also don't have access to many of the benefits that permanently contracted employees do. For example, you're not entitled to redundancy pay if you're laid off, your employer does not have to give you notice before ending your employment, and you will not be eligible to join your employer's pension scheme.

Working a zero hours contract can also be taxing on your social life and work-life balance. Yes, you can turn down shifts you don't want, but if you do this too often your employer may stop asking you. You may find yourself missing social events or struggling to plan your social life because of your unpredictable work pattern.

How to make zero hours contracts work for you

The reality is that, as a student looking for part-time work, you're very likely to encounter zero hours contracts. Here are a few ways you can make them work for you.

Know your rights

Contrary to popular belief, zero hours workers do have some rights. As a zero hours contract worker, you are entitled to:

- The national minimum wage for your age group
- Holiday pay based on the hours you work
- Pay if you're asked to be 'on call'
- Rest breaks at work and between working days or shifts
- Statutory sick pay as long as you earn at least £120 per week (before tax) from that employer on average
- Freedom from bullying, harassment, or unfair treatment based on protected characteristics

The best way to protect your rights at work is to join a trade union for your industry. They can advise you and help you to ensure that your rights are upheld.

Take more than one job

Since 2015, it has been illegal for employers to use exclusivity clauses in zero hours contracts. This means that your employer cannot stop you from having a second job or penalise you for working for somebody else.

So for example, if you wanted to take a Saturday job in a shop and then pick up zero hours contract bar work on other days, you can do that. Many students make ends meet by working more than one part-time job in this way.

Be clear about your availability upfront

When you take a zero hours contract, let your manager (or whoever schedules your shifts) know your class schedule and any other firm commitments. The best way to do this is to put it in writing, such as by sending an email. They might not remember it all, but this should cut down on the number of unsuitable shifts you're offered.

By being clear about your availability and then reliably showing up to work when asked, you show your employer that they can depend on you. This can lead to more hours, if that's what you want.

Take extra hours when they're offered

Many zero hours jobs go through busy and less busy periods. For example, entertainment and hospitality industry jobs are likely to be busier at weekends, and retail gets much busier before Christmas. During these periods, you may be offered additional hours.

If possible, it's a good idea to take these hours when they're offered. You'll earn more money, which can help to make up the shortfall from quieter weeks, and you'll get a reputation as someone who volunteers to pitch in when it's needed.

Take unsociable shifts if you can

This isn't universally true, but unsociable shifts (such as night work, Sundays, and public holidays) can often come with a boost in pay. This might be called 'time and a half' or 'double time'. If you can do so without compromising your health, class schedule, or other commitments, picking up these shifts can give your income a serious boost!

Is it right for you?

Zero hours contracts aren't for everyone, and they are controversial for good reason. But for some people, they can work very well. If you're seeking flexibility and can live with the variable income, working zero hours contract jobs can be a great way to bring in some much-needed cash and get some work experience on your CV while you study.

You know best if this type of work is right for you, so do your research and weigh up the pros and cons before you dive in.

4 October 2021

Employment rights

What are employment rights?

By law, all employees have certain rights – drawn up by various governments over the years – to ensure 'fair' relations between employees and employers.

Statutory rights, those rights endowed by law, form the minimum standard for an employee's treatment in the workplace.

Areas of employment rights

Some of the most prominent employment rights that exist in the UK, include the following:

National Living Wage

All employees in the United Kingdom aged over 23 are entitled to the National Living Wage, which in 2021 was set at £8.91. Those under 23 are entitled to the National Minimum Wage which operates under the same principle but with slightly lower rates for younger workers and those on apprenticeship schemes.

Leave

By law, full time workers are entitled to 28 days annual leave during the year including bank holidays. This leave must be paid at the worker's normal rate of remuneration.

For part time workers, the minimum holiday requirement is calculated to reflect their equivalent proportion of full time working.

The right to statutory maternity leave and statutory maternity pay is set out in Part 8 of the Employment Rights Act 1996 and Part 2 of the Maternity and Parental Leave Regulations 1999. Fathers are also now entitled to two weeks paid paternity leave.

Equal pay and equal treatment

The Equality Act of 2010 repealed and replaced earlier equality legislation. It prohibits discrimination – including in the workplace – in relation to the 'protected characteristics': age, disability, gender reassignment, marriage and civil partnership, pregnancy and maternity, race, religion or belief, sex and sexual orientation.

The Right to Strike

In Britain, employees do not enjoy a right to strike per se. Rather, unions are given statutory immunity from the common law consequences of industrial action, provided certain criteria are met. Employees who then participate in a 'legal' strike are immune from dismissal as otherwise they would typically be in breach of their contract when doing so.

A series of Acts of Parliament from 1906-2016 have granted unions, and union officials, immunity from liability for striking. This is the case as long as unions conduct a secret postal ballot, in which the majority of members (typically with a turnout of 50%) agree to strike action.

Rights around dismissal

There are a number laws and regulations covering the means by which an employee can and cannot be dismissed. For example, under the Employment Relations Act 1999, an employee dismissed for participating in statutorily immune industrial action is regarded as unfairly dismissed.

If an employee is dismissed following a disciplinary process, and the employee believes they have been unfairly dismissed, an employment tribunal will look at whether the employer followed the correct disciplinary procedures.

Employees also have rights in relation to minimum redundancy payments.

Agency work

An agency worker has a contract with an employment agency rather than the hiring firm/organisation.

Once an agency worker has been on assignment in the same role for the same hirer for a period of 12 continuous calendar weeks, they become entitled to the same basic terms of employment as if he or she had been directly recruited by the hirer.

Employment rights around the world

Some examples of how employment rights work around the world include:

France

In France, the standard working week is 35 hours, and under the 2000 Aubry Law, those working above that level are entitled to overtime, or extra time off.

So called gardening leave (where an employee remains under an employment contract prior to termination, but may be released from working), is not permitted. In France this violates the essential principle that it is the employer's responsibility to provide work to the employee.

Companies in France of a certain size are required to operate with a 'Works Council'. Under these arrangements, non-voting employee representatives are entitled to attend meetings of the Board of Directors. They must also be consulted in relation to a number of business changes like a company acquisition or the discontinuation of a product line or division.

Africa

In Angola, maximum daily and weekly working hours are 8 hours per day and 44 hours per week. The minimum wage is established by Presidential Decree.

In Nigeria, normal hours of work are fixed either by mutual agreement, by collective bargaining within the organisation or by an industrial wages board. Overtime must be paid for, but the rate to be paid is not specified by law.

Asia

In China, the maximum number of working hours is 40 hours per week and 8 hours per day, except in the case of a flexible working hour system or a comprehensive working hour system, which requires approval from the local labour authority. The minimum wage is stipulated by local regulations.

In Japan, employers cannot require employees to work for more than 8 hours per day or 40 hours per week

Americas

In the United Sates of America, employers are covered by the Fair Labor Standards Act (FLSA) which guarantees minimum wage and overtime pay for non-exempt employees. There is no federal limit on the number of hours per day or per week that an employee over the age of 16 can work. All non-exempt employees must be paid at least the federal minimum wage, which in 2020 was $12 per hour for companies with under 25 staff, and $13 per hour for those with over 25 staff.

In Argentina, the general maximum number of hours is 8 hours per day or 48 hours per week for all employed workers in public or private enterprises. The national minimum wage is updated regularly by the National Council of Employment dependent of the Ministry of Work, Employment and Social Security (Ministry).

In Columbia, employees must have at least 1 paid day off every 6 days (usually Sundays). The ordinary working day is from 6:00 am to 9:00 pm.

The debate around employment rights

The benefits of employment rights

Employment regulation is designed to counter unfair work practices and ensure income and job security for the UK's workforce.

According to qualitative analysis by the Confederation of British Industry (CBI), offering fair pay and protecting employment rights has a positive impact on trust in business. It also suggests that fairness in employee treatment leads to increased productivity.

A national minimum wage can lead to a 'fairer' distribution of income between the higher paid and the low paid. Poverty may be reduced in turn.

A limit to the capabilities of employers to 'hire and fire' means employees can hold down jobs for longer. This can lead to them gaining greater skills in a particular industry and becoming more productive in the long run.

Greater job security for employees means that they consume in the economy with more confidence. The same logic applies for investment and house-buying, the latter of which has significant social benefits.

While 28% of the CBI's (Confederation of British Industry) membership said employment law was an administrative burden, almost two-thirds of the CBI's membership agreed that 'implementing employment law makes a positive contribution to employee relationships'.

Concerns surrounding employment rights

Critics of expanding employment rights say that while 'fairness' is important, so is a flexible economy, which is said in turn to support economic growth.

Flexibility in the labour market has long been championed as part of the UK's competitive advantage over other nations. It is said to act as a magnet for foreign investment and, in turn, growth, jobs and productivity improvements.

Those supporting a flexible labour market suggest it can be positive for both employees and employers, particularly smaller businesses. Limiting the bureaucracy involved in 'hiring and firing' means that new employees can get jobs quicker and firms can employ more efficiently. They argue that high levels of bureaucracy and costs associated with employment can lead to firms moving their business operations overseas.

Those wary of the encroachment of employment rights warn that significant job security can act as a disincentive to working hard. It is also suggested that strong employment rights can create a time lag between central bank policy and the real economy. This is because firms are forced to take longer to adapt to new interest rate levels or economic conditions due to regulation.

History of employment rights in the UK

19th century

With the industrial revolution well underway, from the middle of the 19th century Acts of Parliament were passed to better protect workers' rights.

- The Factory Act 1833 prohibited the employment of children under 9.

- The Factory Act of 1874 raised the minimum age of employment for children to ten years in textile factories.

- The Employer and Workman Act of 1875 placed employers and employees on equal footing and allowed all breaches of contract to be covered by civil law.

- The Factory and Workshop Act of 1895 further regulated the conditions, safety, health and wages of people working in factories.

1900 – 1945

The Trade Disputes Act 1906 added the famous words to UK employment law: 'An act done in pursuance of an agreement or combination by two or more persons shall, if done in contemplation or furtherance of a trade dispute, not be actionable unless the act, if done without any such agreement or combination, would be actionable'. These are still found in section 219 of the Trade Union and Labour Relations (Consolidation) Act 1992.

The 1970s

Equality in the work place has not always been enforced by law. It wasn't until 1975 with the Sex Discrimination Act that equality began to be introduced into law. This was closely followed in 1976 by the Race Relations Act which was established to prevent race discrimination.

1979 – 1997

The 1980 Employment Act redefined 'lawful picketing'. An 80% majority was required to legalise a 'closed shop', it repealed the statutory recognition procedure and it restricted unfair dismissal and maternity rights.

The 1982 Employment Act placed further restrictions on industrial action. The 80% rule was extended to all closed shops every 5 years, it removed union only labour clauses in commercial contracts and it meant employers could obtain injunctions against unions and sue unions for damages.

The 1986 Public Order Act introduced new criminal offences in relation to picketing.

1997 – 2010

The 1998 National Minimum Wage Act introduced a national minimum wage for those over 18, subject to exceptions for training, volunteer work, residents in charities and religious communities.

The 1998 Working Time Regulations Act implemented a European Commission Directive with respect to maximum working hours.

The 1998 Human Rights Act gave effect to the European Convention on Human Rights in UK law. This included granting better protection from discrimination by public authority.

The 1999 Employee Relations Act amended the Trade Union Labour Relations (Consolidation) Act 1992. Dismissal for participation in official industrial action was deemed unfair within a protected period of 8 weeks.

The Equality Act of 2010 brought together more than 116 separate pieces of legislation into one single act – a new streamlined legal framework to protect the rights of individuals and advance equality of opportunity.

2010 – present day

The 2016 Trade Union Act made it more difficult for workers to engage in industrial action.

In all industrial action ballots, at least 50% of those entitled to vote must now do so, with a majority then in favour of industrial action. If the majority of those entitled to vote are 'normally engaged' in the provision of 'important public services' at least 40% of those 'entitled' to vote must vote in favour of action.

Furthermore, unions now must give 14 days' notice of any industrial action, unless the employer agrees that 7 days' notice is enough (previously 7 days' notice was enough).

Since 2013 claimants have had to pay fees to issue an employment tribunal claim and have it heard, unless they qualify for a reduction or waiver on the grounds of having limited wealth and low income.

Statistics

The UK is one of the safest places to work in the EU. In 2014, the standardised rate of fatal injuries to employees in the UK was 0.55 per 100,000 employees, the lowest of those published by Eurostat.

The number of tribunal cases has dropped since 2010. In 2019/20 the number of cases heard was 103,973, in 2009/10 it was over 236,000.

In 2018, according to the Office of National Statistics, there were 273,000 working days lost due to labour disputes, the sixth-lowest annual total since records began in 1891.

Quotes

'Trade unions stand up for the rights of workers from all countries, regardless of their immigration status or race. Trade unions build solidarity between workers which stops employers dividing workers and driving down conditions'. – Trade Union Congress

'The UK's flexible labour market also acts as a catalyst for innovation. Working flexibly is a positive choice for most people and this should be celebrated' – Confederation of British Industry

Why critical thinking skills matter at work

Our brains make thousands of super-fast assessments and quick calculations every day. Most of these are automatic, we don't even realise it's happening. But sometimes we need to take time to think more pro-actively, carefully weighing up decisions and questioning what we're told.

This is called critical thinking, and it's a vital soft skill to develop for school and work. In this guide we'll look at:

♦ What is critical thinking?

♦ Why is critical thinking important?

♦ Examples of critical thinking.

♦ How to improve critical thinking.

'Critical thinking is one of top 5 skills that employers value. Discover how to develop yours'

What is critical thinking?

Here's the official definition of critical thinking from the Foundation for Critical Thinking:

'Critical thinking is the intellectually disciplined process of actively and skilfully conceptualizing, applying, analysing, synthesising, and/or evaluating information gathered from, or generated by, observation, experience, reflection, reasoning, or communication, as a guide to belief and action.'

Bit of a mouthful, right? If we break that down, the definition of critical thinking is essentially the ability to carefully and deliberately analyse information in order to understand things better.

Critical thinking skills allow you to really evaluate facts and data rather than just accepting them at face value.

Why is critical thinking important?

A LinkedIn survey from 2016 found that critical thinking was one of top 5 skills that employers value. What's more, mentions of critical thinking in job postings have doubled since 2009, according to Indeed.com. So it's a really useful transferable skill to add to your CV.

Efficient and successful staff members know how to think critically. That's because critical thinkers look beyond the basic information they're given, and look at things from different angles. They don't make decisions based on gut feelings. These qualities make for an employee who is able to solve problems and tackle challenges in a logical way.

Critical thinking also means that you have to gather information from lots of different sources and people, so it can help improve your teamwork skills and research abilities. It can also help you come up with new ideas.

Critical thinking skills also matter at school. You'll be able to develop your own opinions, backed up with evidence and facts. Critical thinking leads to much better essays and in-class debates.

Here are a few examples of critical thinking...

♦ A doctor gives a patient a check-up, researches their symptoms and diagnoses an illness.

♦ A lawyer reviews evidence in court and comes up with a strategy to win the case.

♦ A scientist analyses data from the lab to draw conclusions.

♦ A marketing manager evaluates sales data to conclude whether a new product is popular with customers.

Remember this is just a handful of examples –you can apply critical thinking to any career or job role.

How to improve critical thinking

Show employers that you know how to think critically by trying out these techniques to develop your skills...

1. Ask questions

This first step is fairly simple, but it's one a lot of us overlook. When you have a task or are trying to find solutions to a problem, go back to basics. Ask straight-forward questions. What information do you already have? Where did that information come from? What exactly are you trying to solve, prove or explain?

2. Question your basic assumptions

We all have biases about different situations – whether we realise it or not. Before any task, ask yourself, what do I believe about this scenario? Have I already formed any opinions? Take the time to really question all the assumptions you might be making.

3. Examine all the evidence

Are the facts you're being given trust-worthy? What is the original source of that piece of research? Is this data objective? Thoroughly examine and investigate all the information you're working with.

4. Think for yourself!

And finally, it's important to draw your own logical conclusions and not be swayed by what other people think. Test information out and rely on your own powers of critical thinking!

Bullying at work

While bullying may make you think of the school playground, experiencing it is anything but childish. When you're forced to face your tormenter everyday at work it can be serious, exhausting. It might even get to the point where you're considering quitting. We totally get it. But before you hand in your resignation, read this article.

By Nishika Melwani

Bullying at work is a gradual process that wears the victim down, and makes them feel worthless. This can be both in terms of their work as well as their personal life. Sometimes the bully can be one individual, but it can also come from a group. In the worst case scenario, bullying may just be a part of the company's culture. Regardless of where it comes from, bullying and harassment at work is always wrong.

What is bullying at work in the UK?

So, we should probably start by answering the question you've come to this article for – What is bullying at work?

Well, The Andrea Adams Trust, the national charity against workplace bullying, defines it as:

♦ Unnecessary, humiliating behaviour towards an individual or a group of employees either through social media or in person.

♦ Persistent offensive, intimidating and/or malicious attacks on personal or professional performance carried out for a negative purpose or effect. These are often unpredictable and unfair or irrational.

♦ An abuse of power or position that can cause anxiety and distress, or physical ill health.

♦ If someone has taken away your dignity or created an intimidating, hostile atmosphere where people are scared to speak up.

Bullying at work in the UK can be overt, such as physical violence or shouting and swearing, or subtler. For example, ignoring someone, giving them impossible tasks or encouraging malicious gossip about them. And it doesn't matter if you're the hardest-working person in your team; in fact, that may even make you the target of a jealous person.

Employees usually put up with bullying in the workplace because they're afraid of losing their jobs. They might also keep quiet due to a threat from the bully, or because they think it'll escalate the situation.

If you're experiencing bullying at work due to your sexual orientation, race, gender identity or a disability, this is considered discrimination. In fact, it's actually illegal under the Equality Act 2010; you should report it to line managers, or whoever has the authority to help you, as soon as you feel ready.

What to do about workplace bullying

Deflect the bully if you can. Remain calm, stand firm, and try to appear confident. Keep a detailed record of every incident; you'll need it as proof if you decide to make a complaint.

Check your job description. If you suddenly find yourself being set menial tasks, or are given an increased workload with shorter deadlines, that might be a red flag. You can go to senior management and complain if the work you're being asked to do isn't part of your contract.

Try to get witnesses for any bullying incidents. That way you can have solid proof, if you need it, and avoid situations where you are alone with the bully.

Get advice from your trade union, from human resources or health and safety officers at work. Does your employer have a policy on harassment at work? If so, what is it? How do filing a complaint?

Take a stress management course, and do some assertiveness training. They're good for your general health, and will help you in the future. Plus they'll help you feel like you're taking control of the situation.

Pursuing the complaint...

If you go ahead with a complaint, choose your words carefully. State the facts clearly – don't just tear down your coworker's character (as tempting as it might be). You could be accused of malicious behaviour.

Get emotional support from your family and friends. Let them know what's going on and how you're truly feeling about it. You could also ask your GP about counselling and even take sick leave if you need it.

If you decide to leave your job because of the bullying, let your company know exactly why you're resigning. It may help others in the future. You could even suggest that the company should start taking steps to prevent anything like this from happening again.

If you want to pursue a legal claim against your employer, you'll need to get some professional advice. Start by taking advice from your union. If you have a good case, they'll probably take it up on your behalf.

Once you start looking at taking legal action, you have options to consider. These include an industrial employment tribunal, civil claims for personal injury, and sometimes even criminal action.

More help with workplace bullying

Here's some links that might be useful if you, or someone you know, are experiencing bullying in the workplace:

♦ No-one deserves to experience bullying in the workplace. If you're in crisis, The Mix is here to help. Our Crisis Messenger provides free, 24/7 crisis support across the UK. If you're aged 25 or under, you can text THEMIX to 85258.

♦ You might also like to read our expert answer on how to deal with a bully boss on our website.

♦ You could also share your experience of workplace bullying on our discussion boards. Opening up about it is the first step towards putting an end to it.

♦ Acas can also help. They offer free advice about everything to do with employment law, you can call them on 0300 123 1100.

♦ BullyingUK offers advice and support to victims of bullying. Call them on 0808 800 2222.

29 January 2022

When your dream job is a nightmare

An Article from *The Conversation*.

THE CONVERSATION

By Lisa Cohen, Associate Professor, Business Administration, McGill University & Sandra E. Spataro, Professor, Northern Kentucky University

What happens when you land your dream job but it turns out to be anything but?

Friends, career consultants and the media inundate us with a constant barrage of advice telling us to follow our dreams, find our bliss or pursue our passions in our professional lives. Yet this kind of advice is not always easily followed.

Even when it's heeded, the advice can come with downsides, especially when it turns out that those aforementioned passions involve jobs with routine, day-to-day tasks that people are less than passionate about. In short, work is often hard work.

People land jobs in data science and artificial intelligence, for example, expecting to create brilliant algorithms that will solve big problems. But they often end up performing menial data collection and cleaning tasks. The excitement of working for a startup loses its lustre with difficult and boring work often outside an employee's primary areas of interest.

And not everyone promoted to the lauded ranks of management is thrilled to be there performing management tasks, or even see the job as a step up.

People romanticize working in the media, fashion, film, fine and performing arts and other cultural industries, but the work often ends up being more drudgery than glamour. Any job, especially an entry-level position, has elements of drudgery.

'Glossy work' is lacklustre

This gap between expectations and the day-to-day reality of jobs is a phenomenon we've labelled as 'glossy work' in a recently published study.

For the study, we interviewed magazine fact-checkers who worked for high-status organizations in a glamorous industry while performing menial tasks every day. They experienced a kind of dissonance between their work and its setting.

As one fact-checker described it:

'Because you're affiliated with the magazine, people think you're a strange type of royalty no matter how you're affiliated.'

We examined how this phenomenon affects them.

For employees, the glossy work dissonance can spur attempts to change the actual job, frustration and a quick exit from the position. Glossy work also creates a dilemma about how to present the work and themselves to the world. How do they balance their simultaneous needs for self-enhancement and to be fully understood and authentic?

Glossing over mundane work

We find they do so by differentiating their descriptions of their jobs across different audiences. When talking to complete outsiders — people at social gatherings, for example — they focus on the more glamorous aspects: working in journalism and for glossy magazines.

For the high-status writers they collaborate with, they focus on their own expertise and other status markers. And to insiders, they present a more complete view of their work.

Presenting themselves differently depending on who they're talking to can mean that anyone who is not a true insider at the company ends up with a partial or biased view of the work. The full nature of the work is often glossed over, and that's a problem for those considering taking one of these jobs.

When they only hear about the gloss, prospective employees end up with false expectations that tend to fuel the cycle of disappointment.

Potential employees can get around this by doing more careful research on the true nature of the jobs they're considering taking. They should ask questions about the position's day-to-day requirements and consult a range of people who currently have the job or who have previously held it.

What employers can do

'Glossy work' also comes at a cost to employers as they try to manage worker frustration and staff turnover. They can stop this vicious cycle by providing realistic job previews. This doesn't mean they should only show the negative side of work, but they should provide an honest balance of the glamorous and less glamorous aspects of the job.

Employers may also want to consider alternative ways of assembling tasks so that the less pleasant tasks are spread across employees and jobs.

They may also want to be open to employee efforts to craft and tweak their jobs and create new opportunities within their organizations.

Ultimately, however, performing many mundane tasks remains a reality in all jobs despite the promise that AI will eliminate more and more rote chores.

What's more, hiring managers should exercise caution when listing 'passion' as a job requirement. In an analysis of more than 200 interviews for a project on startup hiring, passion was a frequent subject of discussion. Hiring managers looked for it. Potential employees wanted to live their passion.

Yet none of the hiring managers who were looking for passion in their prospective employees could describe how they would assess passion in candidates, or why it was important for the specific job being filled. The risk here is that they hire people who are passionate and then provide work that either doesn't match or douses that passion, creating a problematic situation for both employee and employer.

11 May 2021

Key Facts

- 150 million new technology jobs will be created in the next five years. (Page 3)

- Only 2%-3% of employment applications result in an interview. (Page 5)

- Up to 80% of people secure employment opportunities through networking and personal connections. (Page 6)

- When a good position gets posted online, it receives about 200+ resumes and cover letters from job seekers. (Page 9)

- Most school students will do work experience in Year 10, or occasionally in Year 11. If you go to Sixth Form or a further education college, you might also get a chance to do additional work experience in Year 12. Most placements last one or two weeks. (Page 11)

- 162,000 unemployed young people were in full-time education (35% of all unemployed young people) in November 2021-January 2022. (Page 18)

- The unemployment rate for 16-24 year olds in full-time education was 14.0%, down from 19.5% a year before. (Page 18)

- 22% of all people who had been unemployed for over 12 months were 16-24 year olds. (Page 19)

- Youth unemployment has been an escalating problem in the UK since 2005, with the most recent rises directly attributable to issues of the economy. (Page 20)

- UK businesses struggle to recruit young, work-ready staff. (Page 20)

- With nearly 1 million young people unemployed, that is approximately 1 in 5 young people that are unemployed. (Page 20)

- The unemployment rate for recent graduates in England aged 21 to 30 reached 6.3% in 2020, after it had gradually fallen over nearly a decade since a peak of 6.5% in 2012. (Page 22)

- Despite the rise in unemployment, pay rates held up for graduates who succeeded in finding a job, with graduates aged 21-64 being paid an average salary of £35,000, £9,500 more than their peers who did not go to university and an increase of £500 on 2019. (Page 22)

- Salaries differed by industry and by gender, with men working in banking and finance making the most at £45,000, and women working in hotels and restaurants the least, at £26,500. (Page 22)

- Across the entire workforce there has been a reduction in paid work of between 4 and 4.5 per cent. (Page 23)

- Young people are far more likely than their older counterparts to think it's becoming easier for people from less advantaged backgrounds to move up in British society (35 per cent of 18 to 24 year olds compared with 19 per cent of 25 to 49 year olds). (Page 23)

- According to a recent article in the Financial Times, the percentage of unemployed under-25s rose from 11.5 in February 2020 to 12.95 in June 2021. (Page 24)

- As Europe shut down in March 2020, many jobs were simply removed. Between March and May 2020, there were only 476,000 vacancies in the UK. Compared to the same period in 2019, this means there were 365,000 fewer jobs, a 42 percent decrease. (Page 25)

- By now, the demand-side of the UK-job market has largely recovered from the pandemic. In May to July 2021, there were 953,000 vacancies. This puts the number of vacancies in the UK above its pre-pandemic level. (Page 25)

- According to the Living Wage Foundation, the 'real' living wage is currently £9.90 an hour for workers across the UK and £11.05 in London, almost a pound above the mandatory National Living Wage. (Page 27)

- As of 2021, 917,000 people in the UK work on a zero hours contract. (Page 30)

- By law, full time workers are entitled to 28 days annual leave during the year including bank holidays. (Page 32)

- The right to statutory maternity leave and statutory maternity pay is set out in Part 8 of the Employment Rights Act 1996 and Part 2 of the Maternity and Parental Leave Regulations 1999. Fathers are also now entitled to two weeks paid paternity leave. (Page 32)

- The UK is one of the safest places to work in the EU. In 2014, the standardised rate of fatal injuries to employees in the UK was 0.55 per 100,000 employees, the lowest of those published by Eurostat. (Page 34)

- A LinkedIn survey from 2016 found that critical thinking was one of top five skills that employers value. (Page 35)

Apprenticeship

A form of vocational training which involves learning a trade or skill through working. An apprentice will often shadow an experienced practitioner of a trade, learning the occupation 'on the job'. Some apprenticeships can take many years.

Economy

The way in which a region manages its resources. References to the 'national economy' indicate the financial situation of a country: how wealthy or prosperous it is.

Entrepreneur

An individual who starts and runs their own business.

Flexible working

Any working pattern which allows an individual to vary the time or place in which work is done. Flexible working schemes include part-time work, flexitime and job sharing.

Freelancer

People who work for themselves and contract out their services.

Graduate

Someone who has studied for and been awarded a degree.

Labour market

The market in which workers compete for jobs and employers compete for workers.

Living Wage

The Living Wage is a wage that is based on the cost of living and is set by the Living Wage Foundation. There is a UK rate and a London rate.

Maternity leave

Female employees have the statutory right to a minimum amount of time off during and following a pregnancy. Statutory maternity leave is currently 39 weeks paid, six weeks at 90% of full pay and the remainder at a flat rate (as of 2009 = £123.06), or 90% of your salary if that is less than the flat rate.

Minimum wage

The National Minimum Wage (NMW) is a minimum amount per hour that most workers in the UK are legally entitled to be paid. The level of NMW you are entitled to depends on your age.

National living wage

The national living wage is now £10.20 an hour for those living in London and £8.75 in the rest of the UK. This is the amount that the Government believes is the minimum people need to be paid in order to achieve a basic standard of living in which all necessities can be paid for.

NEET

Young people not in employment, education or training.

Paternity leave

Fathers-to-be who meet certain conditions are entitled to one or two weeks paid paternity leave.

Pay gap

The gender pay gap refers to the difference between men and women's earnings. Currently, women earn on average 21% less than their male counterparts.

Pension

When someone reaches retirement age, they are entitled to receive a regular pension payment from the government. This payment takes the place of a salary. Many people choose to pay into a private pension fund throughout their career, in order to save extra money for when they retire. Often, employers also pay into a pension fund for their employees. The State Pension Age is gradually increasing. The Pensions Act 2011 will see the State Pension Age for both men and women increase to 66 by October 2020 to `keep pace with increases in longevity (people living longer)`.

Recruitment

The process of finding new employees to fill vacancies.

Redundancy

An amount of money paid by an employer when there is no longer the need or capacity for you to remain employed by them.

Retirement

The time in a person's life when they stop work completely.

Secondment

A secondment is a temporary move to another organisation or department, often to carry out a specific project or gain experience.

Service industry

A business that provides goods but does not manufacture them, for example catering.

Vocational

A qualification which is relevant to a particular career and can be expected to provide a route into that career.

Work-life balance

Having a measure of control over when, where and how you work, in order to enjoy an optimal quality of life. In a 2008 survey of Oxbridge graduates, a majority in every sector said they would prioritise work-life balance when thinking about their career.

Activities

Brainstorming

♦ In pairs, discuss what you know about unemployment in the UK. Draw a mind-map of all the things you think about in connection with the issue of unemployment.

♦ In small groups, think about the different types of career paths people might follow after they leave school. List as many careers as you can think of, and include a note that explains whether each job requires a degree, A-levels, GCSEs, work experience, an apprenticeship, a college course, etc.

♦ With a partner, discuss skills that employers may look for in employees. Design a diamond9 chart to rank the employability skills that are important.

♦ In small groups, make a list of jobs that you associate with gender stereotyping and write them in two columns headed 'male' and 'female'. Rank the jobs from highest to lowest earnings in each column and discuss the groups' findings.

♦ In small groups, make a list of 'jobs of the future'; what do you think work may be like in fifty years time?

Research

♦ Pick a career that interests you and research how you can achieve that career. Include training/routes into work and how much you are likely to earn.

♦ Research the way in which the gender pay gap affects people. Write some notes on your findings and feedback to the rest of the class.

♦ Choose a country in Europe and research their attitude to work and employment. Write some notes on your findings and feedback to your class.

♦ Research the opportunities afforded by self-employment, and some careers where being self-employed is an option. Write some notes and feedback to your class.

♦ In small groups, create a questionnaire about future employment. Ask the rest of your class to complete the questionnaire and feedback to your class the results.

♦ Have a look at jobs available in your area. Are there many positions available? Is there much variety in the types of work? Show your findings in a graph.

Design

♦ Create a leaflet that explains the positives and negatives of zero-hours contracts.

♦ Design a poster that will encourage people who are unemployed and not currently seeking work, to look for employment.

♦ Design a poster to persuade people to either go to university or become an apprentice.

♦ Using one of the articles in this book, create a poster to display the main theme of the article.

♦ Design a poster for a 'job of the future'. Be creative!

♦ Create a CV for yourself. Use articles in this book as a guide on what should be included.

Oral

♦ Think about a job you would like to do in the future and create a five-minute presentation that explores the qualifications and experience you might need in order to enter that profession.

♦ Discuss with a partner, what work means to you and how it could improve your personal well-being.

♦ Role-play with a partner an interview for a job in an office. Discuss and make notes afterwards on the positive and negative things that each of you said.

♦ Discuss with someone who is currently employed about their work. Ask them things such as 'How did you get into work?', 'What qualifications did you need?', 'Have you changed career?' Think of your own questions and make notes on their answers.

Reading/writing

♦ Imagine that you are a parent who wishes to return to work after having a baby. Write a letter to your employer requesting flexible working. Include in the letter why you think that they should allow you to do this.

♦ Write a paragraph on where you think you will be in ten-years time. Include a bullet-point list on how you think you will achieve your goals.

♦ Find an advert for a job that may interest you, write a cover letter (using articles in this book to help you) for that job.

♦ Create an advert for a job. Include things such as salary and tasks involved in the job.

Acknowledgements

The publisher is grateful for permission to reproduce the material in this book. While every care has been taken to trace and acknowledge copyright, the publisher tenders its apology for any accidental infringement or where copyright has proved untraceable. The publisher would be pleased to come to a suitable arrangement in any such case with the rightful owner.

The material reproduced in **issues** books is provided as an educational resource only. The views, opinions and information contained within reprinted material in **issues** books do not necessarily represent those of Independence Educational Publishers and its employees.

Images

Cover image courtesy of iStock. All other images courtesy Freepik, Pixabay & Unsplash.

Illustrations

Simon Kneebone: pages 12, 21 & 30. Angelo Madrid: pages 8, 14 & 24.

Additional acknowledgements

With thanks to the Independence team: Shelley Baldry, Tracy Biram and Jackie Staines.

Danielle Lobban

Cambridge, June 2022